GERSHWIN REMEMBERED

Gershwin
Remembered

EDWARD JABLONSKI

faber and faber
LONDON · BOSTON

First published in 1992
by Faber and Faber Limited
3 Queen Square London WC1N 3AU

Phototypeset by Intype, London
Printed in England by Clays Ltd, St Ives Plc

© Edward Jablonski, 1992

Edward Jablonski is hereby identified as author of this work
in accordance with Section 77 of the Copyright, Designs
and Patents Act 1988.

A CIP record for this book is available from the British Library

ISBN 0–571–14130–7
0–571–14131–5 (Pbk)

For
ROBIN RUPLI

Contents

Illustrations

Acknowledgements

I am grateful for permission to quote from the following (provided copyright owners could be located) and for the kind assistance tendered by members of the Gershwin family and friends. The late Ira Gershwin should lead the list because of kindnesses, suggestions and help with Gershwin material over nearly two decades. Other sources: Franklin P. Adams, *The Diary of Our Own Samuel Pepys* (Simon & Schuster, 1935); Merle Armitage (ed.), *George Gershwin* (Longmans, Green & Co., 1938), *George Gershwin – Man and Legend* (Duell, Sloan and, Pearce, 1958); Fred Astaire, *Steps in Time* (Harper & Brothers, 1959); Rudi Blesh, *Shining Trumpets* (Alfred A. Knopf, 1953); Mario Braggiotti (*Etude*, 1953); Gilbert Chase, *America's Music* (McGraw-Hill, 1955); Abram Chasins (*Saturday Review*, 1956); Ralph de Tolendano, *Frontiers of Jazz* (Oliver Durrell, 1947); Ira Gershwin, *Lyrics on Several Occasions* (Alfred A. Knopf, 1959); Marc Gershwin, Frances Gershwin Godowsky, Leopold Godowsky III and Isaac Goldberg, *George Gershwin* (Simon & Schuster, 1931); Edward Jablonski and Lawrence D. Stewart, *The Gershwin Years* (Doubleday & Co., 1958); Constant Lambert, *Music Ho!* (Faber and Faber, 1934); Burton Lane, Ring Lardner and George S. Kaufman, *June Moon* (Charles Scribner's Sons, 1930); Oscar Levant, *A Smattering of Ignorance* (Doubleday, Doran & Co., 1941); Wilfrid Mellers, *Music in a New Found Land* (Alfred A. Knopf, 1965); Beverly Nichols, *Are They the Same at Home?* (George H. Doran Co., 1927); Abbe Niles (*The New Republic*, 1926); Henry O. Osgood, *So This is Jazz* (Little, Brown & Co., 1926); Paul Rosenfeld, *An Hour With American Music* (J. B. Lippincott, 1929); Oliver Saylor, *Revolt in the Arts* (Brentano's, 1930); Mabel Schirmer and Gilbert Seldes, *The 7 Lively Arts*, (reprint, with additions and emendations, of 1924 edn; Sagamore Press, 1957); Charles G. Shaw, *The Low-Down* (Henry Holt & Co., 1928); Lawrence D. Stewart, Kay Swift and Carl Van Vechten (*Vanity Fair*, 1925); Ralph Vaughan Williams, *The Making of Music*, (Cornell University Press, 1955); Paul Whiteman and Mary Margaret

McBride, *Jazz* (J. H. Sears & Co., 1926); Alexander Woolcott (*Hearst's International Cosmopolitan*, 1933).

The Gershwin–Heyward letters were given to me by Dorothy Heyward in 1958 at the time Lawrence Stewart and I were working on *The Gershwin Years*, where they appeared initially though in a different arrangement – as also in my recent *Gershwin*. The letters to Isaac Goldberg, deposited in the Harvard University, were also used in both of the Gershwin books on which I worked. I am grateful to Leopold Godowsky III for others and, not the least, to Mabel Schirmer.

The illustrations, unless otherwise identified, are from my own Gershwin Archive photo collection accumulated over several years with the help of Ira Gershwin, Lawrence D. Stewart, Stanley Green, Maurice Levine and others.

Introduction

More than fifty years after his death George Gershwin is widely admired as a remarkably vital, dynamic and richly gifted personality. His music is loved and celebrated as if untouched by the tragedy of his early death. Gershwin's admirers include musicians, especially composers and pianists; musicians with an academic training Gershwin never had are captivated by his personal inventive touches, melodically, rhythmically and harmonically. Gershwin has definitely become that 'American Composer' that he so longed to be; even perhaps 'The Great American Composer'. This in barely two decades of professional life.

The rediscovery of *Porgy and Bess* as an opera (not a mere musical entertainment), new performances and recordings of the compositions neglected in his lifetime: the *Second Rhapsody, Cuban Overture*, the *'I got rhythm' Variations*, his own *Porgy and Bess Suite* (retitled *Catfish Row*), the newly retrieved songs – these all add to his growing stature.

His miniature masterpieces, especially those songs graced with lyrics by his brother Ira, were greatly admired (as evidenced by several articles in this collection), even by those critics who rejected the concert works. But even the neglected Gershwin rarities, songs that were stuffed into cartons after a show closed or failed, are being 're-discovered' and re-evaluated, even published. Found-again 'production numbers' reveal the composer as a master of choral writing (evident since his first major musical, *Lady, be Good!* in 1924 and achieving full flowering in *Porgy and Bess*). The restoration of the original orchestrations – in the musicals as well as the orchestral works – brings out their true, Gershwinesque, sound: one of endearing charm, haunting lines and twinkling wit.

Gershwin, as many of the early articles devoted to him prove, did not suddenly appear on the musical scene in 1924. Four years *before* the *Rhapsody in Blue* an interviewer expressed the view that Gershwin's 'words seemed more suited to the learned lecturer than to a composer of popular hits'. In 1920 he spoke of the special sound of 'American music' that he wished to express in his own work. At that stage, too, he intimated an eventual attempt at opera.

His youth, his self-assurance, the delight in his own creations, frequently led to a misreading of his personality; his lesser rivals called him arrogant and egocentric. Indeed, early in life he set his eye on a goal and concentrated on it to the neglect of his personal life and, perhaps, happiness. Yet he had a wide, diverse circle of friends and associations that lasted a lifetime. He was popular among women, though, to the perplexity of many, he never married (he talked about it, however, in the troubled final year of his life). But work was all to Gershwin; he lived in his music. The pieces, views and quotations in this collection (many long out of print, many never published before) may be helpful in understanding why.

Edward Jablonski, New York, May 1992

Chronology

Gershwin's Life and Works
Contemporary Figures and Events

1898   *26 September* George Gershwin (né Jacob Gershwine) born Brooklyn, New York

1898   Hemingway, Brecht, Paul Robeson, Henry Moore born
Aubrey Beardsley (26), Lewis Carrol (66), die
First performances of *Ein Heldenleben* (R. Strauss), *Sadko* (Rimsky-Korsakov)
Ballad of Reading Goal Wilde
The Curies discover radium
Spanish–American War

1899   Noël Coward, Alfred Hitchcock, Poulenc born
First performances of *Enigma Variations* (Elgar), *Maple Leaf Rag* (Scott Joplin), *Verklärte Nacht* (Schoenberg)
Aspirin is invented
Outbreak of Boer War

1900   *14 March* Birth of brother Arthur

1900   Copland, Weill born
Sullivan (58) dies
First performances of *Tosca* (Puccini), *Finlandia* (Sibelius)
Chekhov, *Uncle Vanya*; Freud, *The Interpretation of Dreams*
Planck formulates quantum theory

1901   Walt Disney, Jascha Heifetz born
Toulouse-Lautrec (37), Verdi (88) die
First performances of *Russalka* (Dvořák), Piano Concerto No. 2 (Rachmaninov)
Queen Victoria dies
First Nobel Prizes awarded
Thomas Mann, *Buddenbrooks*

1902   Marlene Dietrich, John Steinbeck, Walton born
Samuel Butler (67), Zola (62) die
First performances of *Pelléas et Mélisande* (Debussy), Second Symphony (Sibelius)
End of Boer War

1903   Lennox Berkeley, Khachaturian, Evelyn Waugh born
Paul Gaugin (55) dies
Shaw, *Man and Superman*
The Wright brothers fly the first heavier-than-air flying machine

	Richard Steiff creates first 'teddy bears' named after President Theodore Roosevelt

1904   Balanchine, Dali, Dallapiccola, Graham Greene born
        Chekhov (44), Dvořák (63) die
        First performances of *Jenůfa* (Janáček), *Madam Butterfly* (Puccini)
        Barrie, *Peter Pan*
        Rolls-Royce Company founded

1905   Constant Lambert, Tippett, Sartre born
        First performances of *La Mer* (Debussy), *The Merry Widow* (Lehár), *Salome* (Strauss)
        Einstein published his *Special Theory of Relativity*
        Russian ('Bloody Sunday') Revolution

1906   *December* Birth of sister Frances ('Frankie') on the tenth birthday of brother Ira (b. 6 December 1896)

1906   Shostakovich, Beckett born
        Cézanne (67), Ibsen (78) die
        Elgar, *The Kingdom*
        San Francisco earthquake

1907   Auden, Moravia born
        Grieg (64) dies
        First performances of *A Village Romeo and Juliet* (Delius)

1908   Meets Maxie Rosenzweig (later violin virtuoso Max Rosen)

1908   Elliot Carter, Messiaen, Simone de Beauvoir born
        Rimsky-Korsakov (64) dies
        First performances of *Brigg Fair* (Delius), First Symphony (Elgar), *Poem of Ecstasy* (Scriabin)

1909   Stephen Spender, Robert Helpmann born
        Albéniz (48) dies
        First performances of Third Piano Concerto (Rachmaninov), *Elektra* (Strauss)
        Bleriot flies across the English Channel
        Henry Ford's Model 'T' launched
        Bakelite invented

1910   Jean Genet, Samuel Barber born
        Balakirov (73), Tolstoy (82), Mark Twain (75) die

First performances of String Quartet (Berg), *Firebird* (Strav-
insky), *A Sea Symphony* and *Fantasia on a Theme by Thomas
Tallis* (Vaughan Williams)
Union of South Africa

1911   Menotti born
W. S. Gilbert (75), Mahler (50) die
First performances of *Der Rosenkavalier* (Strauss), *Petrushka*
(Stravinsky), 'Alexander's Ragtime Band' Irving Berlin
Bruno Walter conducts posthumous first performance of
Mahler's *Das Lied von der Erde*
Amundsen reaches South Pole

1912   Begins to study piano with Charles Hambitzer

1912   Cage, Ionesco born
Massenet (70) dies
First performances of *Daphnis et Chloë* (Ravel), *Pierrot
lunaire* (Schoenberg)
Titanic sinks on maiden voyage
Scott's last expedition to the South Pole

1913   Enters the High School of Commerce

1913   Britten, Camus, Lutoslawski born
First performances of *Gurrelieder* (Schoenberg), *Le sacre du
printemps* (Stravinsky), 6 Orchestral Pieces (Webern)
D. H. Lawrence, *Sons and Lovers*; Thomas Mann, *Death in
Venice*

1914   Dylan Thomas, Tennessee Williams born
Joyce, *The Dubliners*
Outbreak of First World War

1915   Begins recording piano rolls

1915   Saul Bellow, Arthur Miller, Sviatoslav Richter born
Rupert Brooke (28), Scriabin (43) die
Somerset Maugham, *Of Human Bondage*
First New York to San Francisco telephone line
Lusitania sunk

1916   Signs contract with the Harry Von Tilzer Publishing Co. for
his first published song, 'When you want 'em, you can't get

'em, when you've got 'em, you don't want 'em' (lyric: Murray Roth)

1916   Milton Babbitt, Yehudi Menuhin born
George Butterworth (31), Granados (48), Henry James (73) die
First performances of *Nights in the Gardens of Spain* (Falla), *Goyescas* (Granados), *Scythian Suite* (Prokofiev)
Battles of Verdun, the Somme, Jutland

1917   *c. January* Remick publishes *Rialto Ripples*, a piano rag, written with Will Donaldson

October/November Rehearsal pianist for *Miss 1917*; meets Victor Herbert and Jerome Kern

December Collaborating with Ira on 'You are not the girl', Remick's contract for 'You-oo, just you' (lyric: Irving Caesar); it is interpolated into *Hitchy-Koo* of 1918

1917   Lou Harrison, Robert Lowell born
Degas (83), Scott Joplin (48) die
First performances of *Arlechino* and *Turandot* (Busoni), *La Rondine* (Puccini), *Leave it to Jane* (Jerome Kern)
Jung, *The Unconscious*
Bolshevik Revolution in Russia

1918   *February* Joins the staff of T. B. Harms as composer

September Harms publishes its first Gershwin song, 'Some Wonderful Sort of Someone' (lyric: Schuyler Greene)

October 'The real American folk song (is a rag)', first George and Ira Gershwin collaboration used in a musical, *Ladies First*

December Gershwin's first musical, *Half Past Eight*, opens and quickly closes, in Syracuse, NY

1918   Bernstein born
Lili Boulanger (24), Debussy (55), Klimt (56), Wilfred Owen (25), Parry (70) die
First performances of *Yip, Yip, Yaphank* (Berlin), First Symphony ('Classical') (Prokofiev), *Histoire du soldat* (Stravinsky)
Spengler, *The Decline of the West*
End of First World War

1919	*May* First full-scale musical, *La-La-Lucille* (lyrics: Arthur Jackson and B. G. DeSylva), opens on Broadway. *Lullaby* for string quartet around this time
1919	Leoncavallo (61), Adeline Patti (77), Renoir (78) die First performances of *Ziegfeld Follies* (Berlin), Cello Concerto (Elgar), Fifth Symphony (Sibelius) Alcock and Brown make first non-stop transatlantic flight Lady Astor first woman to take seat in parliament Treaty of Versailles
1920	*January* Al Jolson records 'Swanee' (lyric: Irving Caesar) *June* Provides the score for *George White's Scandals* (the first of five by Gershwin in this series of revues)
1920	Fricker, Maderna, Charlie Parker born Bruch (82), Modigliani (36) die First performances of *Sally* (Jerome Kern), *Le boeuf sur le toit* (Milhaud), *Le tombeau de Couperin* (Ravel) Sinclair Lewis, *Main Street* First session of the League of Nations, London 19th Amendment to the US Constitution: women have the right to vote
1921	Peter Ustinov born Caruso (48), Saint-Saëns (86) die First performances of *Le Roi David* (Honegger), *Kát'a Kabanová* (Janáček), *Chout*, Third Piano Concerto, *Love for Three Oranges* (Prokofiev), Symphony of Wind Instruments (Stravinsky) Dos Passos, *Three Soldiers* Discovery of insulin by Frederick Banting and Charles Best, Canada Adolf Hitler becomes president of the Nationalist Socialist German Workers Party
1922	*August* Composes his one-act opera *Blue Monday* (libretto and lyrics: B. G. DeSylva) for 1922 *Scandals*
1922	Kingsley Amis, Lukas Foss, Judy Garland, Xenakis born Nikisch (66), Proust (51) die T. S. Eliot, *The Waste Land*; James Joyce, *Ulysses*, Sinclair Lewis, *Babbit* BBC founded

1923   *April The Rainbow* opens in London (lyrics: Clifford Grey)

        1 November Accompanies Eva Gauthier in the 'American' portion of her 'Recital of Ancient and Modern Music for Voice', Aeolian Hall, New York

1923   First peformances of Sonata No. 2 for violin and piano, Dance Suite (Bartók), *Psalmus Hungaricus* (Kodály), *Les noces* (Stravinsky), *Hyperprism* (Varèse)
      Tokyo and Yokohama devastated by major earthquake
      Hitler arrested after failed *putsch* attempt in Munich

1924   *3 January* Paul Whiteman announces 'An Experiment in Modern Music', to be presented at the Aeolian Hall, New York, on 12 February

        21 January Sweet Little Devil (lyrics: B. G. DeSylva) opens in New York

        c. 25 January Completes two-piano version of *Rhapsody in Blue* (Whiteman's arranger–orchestrator, Ferde Grofé, prepares the orchestration)

        10 June Records an abridged *Rhapsody in Blue* with Paul Whiteman and his Concert Orchestra

        11 September Primrose (lyrics: Desmond Carter and Ira Gershwin) opens at the Winter Garden, London

        October/November Works with Ira on a musical for Fred and Adele Astaire then entitled *Black-Eyed Susan*

        1 December Lady, be Good! (*Black-Eyed Susan*) opens at the Liberty Theatre, New York

1924   Lauren Bacall, James Baldwin, Nono born
      Busoni (58), Joseph Conrad (67), Fauré (79), Kafka (41), Puccini (66) die
      First performances of *Pacific 231* (Honegger), *The Cunning Little Vixen* (Janáček), *The Pines of Rome* (Respighi), *Erwartung* (Schoenberg)
      E. M. Forster, *A Passage to India*
      André Breton, *Manifesto of Surrealism*

1925   Begins a notebook labelled 'Preludes', which includes ideas for solo piano pieces, plus 'Nouvelettes'

13 April Tell Me More (lyrics: Ira Gershwin and B. G. DeSylva) opens at the Gaiety; closes after a brief run

22 May Gauthier's 'From Java to Jazz' recital, Aeolian Hall, London; Gershwin accompanies the 'jazz' group

26 May Tell Me More opens at the Winter Garden, London, and is a great success

20 July Gershwin is the first American composer to be featured on the cover of *Time Magazine*

3 December First performance of the Concerto in F, Carnegie Hall, Walter Damrosch conducting the New York Symphony Orchestra, George Gershwin, piano soloist

28 December Tip-toes opens at the Liberty; a success

29 December Paul Whiteman conducts *135 Street* (his name for the one-act opera *Blue Monday*) at Carnegie Hall

30 December Song of the Flame opens at the Forty-Fourth Street Theatre; a huge success

1925   Berio, Boulez born
Satie (59), John Singer Sargent (69) die
First performances of *Wozzeck* (Berg), *Doctor Faust* (Busoni), *No, No, Nanette* (Vincent Youmans)
F. Scott Fitzgerald, *The Great Gatsby*; Kafka, *The Trial*
Hindenburg elected German President

1926   *11 April* Attends a Paul Whiteman concert with the Schirmers, Albert Hall, London; does not approve of Whiteman's interpretation of *Rhapsody in Blue*

14 April Lady, be Good!, starring the Astaires, opens at the Empire Theatre, London

19–20 April Records several of his songs from *Lady, be Good!* with the Astaires for the Columbia Phonograph Co.

6 July Records songs from *Tip-toes*, London; returns to US

31 August Tip-toes opens at the Winter Garden, London

September Reads DuBose Heyward's novel *Porgy*

8 November Oh, Kay!, starring Gertrude Lawrence and Victor Moore, opens at the Imperial, New York

6 December Attends a performance of *The Pirates of Penzance*

1926   Morton Feldman, Hans Werner Henze born
            Firbank (40), Monet (86), Rilke (51) die
            First performances of *The Makropoulos Affair* (Janáček),
            Façade (Sitwell–Walton)
            Hemingway, *The Sun Also Rises*
            Transatlantic radio telephone established
            Germany admitted to the League of Nations
            General Strike in Britain

1927   *21 April* Records first electrical recording of *Rhapsody in Blue* for RCA Victor with the Paul Whiteman Orchestra. Because of disagreements between composer and conductor over tempos, Whiteman stalks out of the studio and the recording is eventually conducted by Nat Shilkret

25 April Gershwin makes his first attempt at a watercolour, a still life

25 July First appearance at an outdoor concert in Lewisohn Stadium, New York. Performs *Rhapsody in Blue*, Willem Van Hoogstraten conducting

5 September Strike up the Band begins Philadelphia try-out prior to New York première; it closes after two weeks, a failure

21 September Oh, Kay!, starring Gertrude Lawrence and Harold French, opens at His Majesty's Theatre, London

October Working with Ira on the songs for *Smarty*, for Fred and Adele Astaire

22 November Smarty, now entitled *Funny Face*, opens to great acclaim at the Alvin Theatre

1927   Gunther Grass, Leontyne Price, Rostropovich born
                Isadora Duncan (47) dies
                First performances of *Show Boat* (Jerome Kern), *Jonny spielt auf* (Krenek), Fourth Piano Concerto (Rachmaninov), *Oedipus Rex* (Stravinsky)
                Sinclair Lewis, *Elmer Gantry*
                First full-length talking film, *The Jazz Singer*, with Al Jolson
                Lindbergh flies solo across the Atlantic
                Alleged anarchists Sacco and Vanzetti executed in Massachusetts

1928   *10 January Rosalie*, starring Marilyn Miller, opens at the New Amsterdam Theatre; Ira's collaborator on the lyrics is P. G. Wodehouse

                7 March Meets Ravel at Eva Gauthier's party

                10 March The Gershwins (George, Ira, Leonore and Frankie) board the *Majestic*, bound for Britain

                19 March Opening night of *That's a Good Girl*, starring Jack Buchanan, at the Hippodrome, London. The lyrics are by Ira Gershwin, Douglas Furber and Desmond Carter; music is by Joseph Meyer and Philip Charig

                22 March 'George Gershwin Night' at the Kit Kat Club

                23 March George and Frankie lunch with Noël Coward; attend his *This Year of Grace*

                25 March To Paris

                27 March The Kolisch Quartet and Gershwin's friend, pianist Josefa Rosanska (Kolisch's wife), meet in the Majestic Hotel; the Quartet performs Schubert and Schoenberg

                3 April Gershwin shops with Mabel Schirmer; on the Avenue de la Grand Armée they also select four taxi-horns he plans to work into his new composition

                8 April Visits Sergei Prokofiev with his friend Vladimir Dukelsky (whom Gershwin renames Vernon Duke)

                16 April Attends a Ballets Russes performance of *Rhapsody in Blue* (choreography by Anton Dolin)

24 April Meets Kurt Weill in Berlin

28 April To Vienna and lunch with Emmerich Kalman

29 April Lunch with Kalman and Ferenc Molnar; sees Krenek's *Jonny spielt auf*, a 'jazz' opera

3 May Meets Franz Lehár and Alban Berg

5 May Hears a performance of the Berg String Quartet

31 May Visited by critic Ernest Newman

8 June Records the Three Preludes and the slow theme from *Rhapsody in Blue* in London

13 June The Gershwins leave for Southampton

18 June Arrives in New York with sketches for *An American in Paris*

1 August Completes the two-piano version of *American in Paris*; working with Ira on *Treasure Girl*, to star Gertrude Lawrence

8 November Treasure Girl opens at the Alvin Theatre, a failure; closes after only 68 performances

12 November Records four songs for Columbia Records, New York

13 December Première of *An American in Paris*, 'a tone poem for orchestra', by the New York Philharmonic, Walter Damrosch conducting, at Carnegie Hall

1928   Stockhausen born
            Thomas Hardy (87), Janáček (75) die
            First performances of *Boléro* (Ravel), *Apollon musagète, Le baiser de la fée* (Stravinsky), *Die Dreigroschenoper* (Weill)
            Museum of Modern Art, New York, founded
            D. H. Lawrence, *Lady Chatterley's Lover* published in Paris; Shaw, *The Intelligent Woman's Guide to Socialism and Capitalism*

1929   *7 April* Watercolour, the self-portrait *Me*, which he presents to composer Harold Arlen

June George, Ira and Gus Kahn (lyrics) work on a show for Florenz Ziegfeld, *Show Girl*, to star Ruby Keeler, the wife of Al Jolson

2 July Show Girl opens at the Ziegfeld, closes after 111 performances

1929 George Crumb, Jacques Brel born
    First performances of *The Rio Grande* (Lambert), *Wake Up and Dream* (Porter), *The Gambler* and *The Prodigal Son* (Prokofiev), *Sir John in Love* (Vaughan Williams)
    Hemingway, *A Farewell to Arms*; Remarque, *Im Westen nichts Neus*
    Graf Zeppelin completes around the world flight
    Wall Street crash
    Trotsky exiled from Russia

1930 *14 January Strike up the Band*, Gershwin conducting, opens at the Times Square Theatre, New York; it runs for 191 performances

14 October Girl Crazy opens at the Alvin Theatre; Gershwin conducts first night. A success, it stars Ginger Rogers and introduces a new star, Ethel Merman. The show runs for 272 performances

1 November Frankie Gershwin marries Leopold Godowsky II, musician (son of the pianist Godowsky I) and one of the developers of Kodachrome

5 November George, Ira and Leonore Gershwin leave for Hollywood

1930 Stephen Sondheim born
    D. H. Lawrence (45), Cosima Wagner (93) die
    First performances of *From the House of the Dead* (Janáček), *Christophe Colomb* (Milhaud), *The New Yorkers* (Porter), *Ever Green* (Richard Rodgers–Lorenz Hart), *Symphony of Psalms* (Stravinsky)
    William Faulkner, *As I Lay Dying*; Dashiell Hammett, *The Maltese Falcon*
    Economic crisis reaches Europe
    Ghandi leads 'march to the sea' in protest at salt tax

1931   *16 January* Works on a 'Manhattan Rhapsody' for the nearly
completed film *Delicious*, starring Janet Gaynor and Charles
Farrell

19 March To Philadelphia to attend the American première
of Berg's *Wozzeck*, Leopold Stokoswki conducting the Grand
Opera Company

10 August All-American concert at Lewisohn Stadium, Fritz
Reiner conducting. Gershwin performs in the *Rhapsody in
Blue*; other composers on the programme: Deems Taylor,
Robert Russell Bennett, whose March for two pianos is played
by William Daly and Oscar Levant

September–October Works on score of *Of Thee I Sing* and a
collection of his own special arrangements of several songs
for piano

30 December Delicious released after delays; one of the earliest
musical films, it is not a success at the Roxy

26 December Of Thee I Sing, from a book by George S.
Kaufman and Morrie Ryskind (lyrics: Ira) opens at the Music
Box. Gershwin conducts the first performance; the satirical
operetta is widely hailed and runs for 441 performances

1931   Leslie Caron born
Bix Beiderbecke (28), d'Indy (80), Melba (70), Nielsen (67)
die
First performances of *Belshazzar's Feast* (Walton), *America's
Sweetheart* (Rodgers–Hart)
Pearl Buck, *The Good Earth*
Empire State Building, New York, completed

1932   *29 January* Première of the *Second Rhapsody*, Gershwin at
the piano, with the Boston Symphony, Serge Koussevitzky
conducting, Boston

2 May George Gershwin's Song-book published by Simon &
Schuster (also known as *Piano Transcriptions of 18 Songs*), in
the composer's arrangements

1 June Ira, George S. Kaufman, Morrie Ryskind awarded

the Pulitzer Prize for *Of Thee I Sing*; at this time there is no prize for music

16 August First performance of *Rumba* by the New York Philharmonic, Albert Coates conducting, Lewisohn Stadium

1 November Conducts the *Cuban Overture* with the Musicians Symphony Orchestra at the Metropolitan Opera House

10 November Appears on the Rudy Vallee Radio Hour performing the Second Prelude and several songs

1932   *Face the Music* (Berlin), *Gay Divorce* (Porter), Piano Concerto in G, Piano Concerto for the left hand (Ravel)
Aldous Huxley, *Brave New World*
Amelia Earhart is first woman to fly solo over the Atlantic
Neutrons discovered

1933   *20 January Pardon My English* opens

22 February Pardon My English closes

22 October Let 'em Eat Cake (libretto: G. S. Kaufman and Morrie Ryskind) opens at the Imperial Theatre; poorly received, it closes after 90 performances

26 October Signs a contract with the Theatre Guild for an opera based on Dorothy and DuBose Heyward's play, *Porgy*

1933   Penderecki, Janet Baker born
Duparc (86) dies
First performances of 'Stormy Weather' (Arlen–Koehler), *As Thousands Cheer* (Berlin), *Roberta* (Kern), *Arabella* (Strauss)
Stein, *Autobiography of Alice B. Toklas*
Hitler appointed Chancellor of Germany by Hindenburg

1934   *15 January* Begins a national tour in celebration of the tenth anniversary of *Rhapsody in Blue*. Première of the *Variations*, Symphony Hall, Boston, Charles Previn conducting the Reisman Symphonic Orchestra, Gershwin at the piano

19 February Begins broadcasting a 15–minute radio series, 'Music by Gershwin', twice a week, Mondays and Fridays, via the National Broadcasting System

August Works on *Porgy* at the Mosbacher home in White Plains, NY, and Fire Island

27 August Life Begins at 8:40 opens at the Winter Garden, with music by Harold Arlen and lyrics by Ira and E. Y. Hatburg

30 September 'Music by Gershwin', second series, an hour-long Sunday broadcast via Columbia Broadcasting System

23 December Final 'Music by Gershwin' broadcast

29 December Guest at the White House with friend Kay Halle; plays for President Franklin D. Roosevelt

1934   Birtwistle, Van Cliburn born
        Delius (72), Elgar (76), Holst (60) die
        First performances of Fifth Symphony (Bax), *Lady Macbeth of Mtsensk* (Shostakovich), *Four Saints in Three Acts* (Virgil Thomson)
        Stalin's 'Purge Trial'

1935   *26 August Porgy* rehearsals begin in New York

        30 September Première of *Porgy and Bess* at the Colonial Theatre, Boston, starring Todd Duncan and Anne Brown in the title roles, Alexander Smallens conducting

        10 October Porgy and Bess opens, to mixed reviews, at the Alvin Theatre, New York

1935   Elvis Presley born
        Berg (50), Dukas (70), T. E. Lawrence (47) die
        First performances of *Die schweigsame Frau* (Strauss)
        Lindbergh and Carrel devise an artificial heart
        Hitler renounces Versailles Treaty
        Italy invades Abyssinia

1936   *21 January* Première of a *Porgy and Bess* orchestral suite (later retitled by Ira Gershwin, as *Catfish Row*), Academy of Music, Philadelphia, Philadelphia Orchestra, Alexander Smallens conducting. Gershwin also appears as soloist in the Concerto in F

21 April Some of his paintings are shown at an exhibition by the Society of Independent Artists

14 May Arthur Lyons, an agent, arranges for the Gershwins to score a Fred Astaire–Ginger Rogers film, *Watch Your Step*

26 June Contract with RKO for two musicals

28 October RKO takes up option on a second Astaire picture

17 November Meets with playwright Lynn Riggs about possible musical to be made from Riggs's American–Mexican drama, *The Lights of Lamy*

14–15 December Concert with the Seattle (Washington) Symphony

1936   Richard Rodney Bennett, Steven Reich born
Glazunov (70), Kipling (71), Lorca (37), Respighi (56) die
First performances of *Mood in Six Minutes* (Harold Arlen), *Top Hat* (Berlin), Third Symphony (Rachmaninov)
Modern Times (Chaplin)
The *Volkswagen* launched
Abdication of Edward VIII
Spanish Civil War

1937   *10–11 February* Appears with the Los Angeles Philharmonic in an all-Gershwin concert, Alexander Smallens conducting; during the rehearsal Gershwin experiences vertigo; during the evening performance he fumbles a passage in the Concerto in F

March He and Ira work on the Astaire (without Rogers) film, *A Damsel in Distress*

12 May Gershwins begin work on songs for *The Goldwyn Follies*

9 June Dizzy spell; medical examination reveals nothing

23–26 June At Cedars of Lebanon Hospital, Los Angeles; Gershwin refuses to take a spinal tap

4 July Leaves 1019 N. Roxbury Drive to settle in vacant home of lyricist E. Y. Harburg

9 July Slips into a coma; rushed to Cedars of Lebanon

10 July Physicians, suspecting a brain tumour, decide on 'energetic surgical intervention' – a five-hour operation for a brain tumour

11 July Sunday, 10.35 a.m., Gershwin dies

1937   Peter Maxwell Davies, Philip Glass born
              Pierné (74), Ravel (62), Roussel (68), Szymanowski (53) die
              First performances of *Music for Strings, Percussion and Celeste*
              (Bartók), *Lulu* (Berg), *Amelia Goes to the Ball* (Menotti),
              Fifth Symphony (Shostakovich)
              Steinbeck, *Of Mice and Men*
              Dupont patents nylon
              German bombers strike Guernica, Spain
              Picasso paints *Guernica*

I

Boyhood and Musical Training

George Gershwin was born in Brooklyn, New York, on 26 September 1898. His father, Morris Gershovitz, was born in St Petersburg, which he left some time in the 1890s to avoid conscription in the Tsar's army. He was initially a designer of 'fancy uppers' for women's shoes. Gershwin recalled that, 'The only creative ancestry that I had seems to have been my father's father who, he tells me, was an inventor in Russia . . . his ingenuity had something to do with the Tsar's guns.' Gershwin's mother, Rose Bruskin, also of St Petersburg, was the daughter of a furrier. The Bruskins preceded Morris to the United States, where they, as would he, settled in the Lower East Side of Manhattan; Rose and Morris were married there on 21 July 1895.

IRA GERSHWIN

(1896–1983)

Born in New York's Lower East Side, Ira Gershwin was
the first of four children born to Rose and Morris Gershwin. He was regarded as the family scholar and his early
education pointed toward a career in one of the professions
– teaching, for example. But while in college, he encount-
ered calculus and 'decided to call it an education'. In his
teens he became a devotee of Gilbert and Sullivan and
revealed a talent for light verse and cartooning. Since his
brother had already left school for Tin Pan Alley, Ira
was exposed to songwriting and songwriters and began
dabbling in the art himself while employed in one of
his father's businesses, a Russian–Turkish bath house in
Harlem. His brother set one of the lyrics to music, though
Ira used the pen name 'Arthur Francis' (after his sister
and youngest brother), so as not to be accused of riding
into Tin Pan Alley on his brother's coat tails. That was in
1918; after some additional collaboration and false starts,
the brothers created their first full score for *Lady, be Good!*
(1924); this unique partnership lasted through George
Gershwin's lifetime. Besides his brother, Ira Gershwin
worked under his own name with several major composers,
among them Vincent Youmans and Vernon Duke. After
his brother's death Ira Gershwin wrote brilliant lyrics for
songs by Jerome Kern, Kurt Weill, Aaron Copland and
Harold Arlen. He retired from songwriting in the mid-
fifties to devote his time to preserving and annotating the
papers and manuscripts for presentation to the Gershwin
Collection, Library of Congress, Washington, DC. His
one book, *Lyrics on Several Occasions*, was published in
1959.

My brother . . . was the second of four children of Morris and Rose
Bruskin Gershwin. I was the oldest, then came George, then Arthur
and last, our sister Frances. Most of our early childhood was spent
on the Lower East Side of Manhattan where my father engaged in
various activities: restaurants, Russian and Turkish baths, bakeries, a
cigar store and pool parlor on the 42nd Street side of what is now

Grand Central Station, book-making at the Brighton Beach Race Track for three exciting but disastrous weeks. When my father sold a business and started another we would inevitably move to a new neighborhood. George and I once counted over twenty-five flats and apartments we remembered having lived in during those days.

Ira Gershwin, 'My Brother', *George Gershwin*, Merle Armitage, ed. (New York, 1938), p. 16

ISAAC GOLDBERG
(1887–1938)

> Gershwin's first biographer, Goldberg was a philologist, musicologist and lecturer at Harvard University. He wrote music criticism for the *American Mercury*; his books include *The Story of Gilbert and Sullivan* and *The Wonder of Words*.

George, as he himself will remind you, was the rough-and-ready, the muscular, type and not one of your sad contemplative children. He was the athletic champion of his gang. His real keyboard was the sidewalks – and, even more, the pavements – of New York . . . Here he revelled in games of 'cat' and hockey; here he achieved his first pre-eminence as the undisputed roller-skating champion of Seventh Street.

Isaac Goldberg, *George Gershwin* (New York, 1931), p. 53

FRANCES GERSHWIN GODOWSKY
(b. 1906)

> The youngest Gershwin and the first to go into the theatre as a dancer–singer, Frances Gershwin married Leopold Godowsky, Jun., son of the famous pianist. Mother of four, she is an accomplished painter. During the 1920s she was a favourite singer of her brothers' songs at parties. In 1973 she recorded a charming album of Gershwin songs.

George was a pretty wild boy. People used to say, 'Mrs Gershwin has nice children, but that son of hers, she's going to have trouble with that son, George.' And they felt sorry for her. I heard he was an independent kid, on his own a lot. He did not have much to do with Ira or Arthur. I don't remember much about his boyhood, though. Remember, I was only about two when we got the piano on Second Avenue and he started lessons.

Frances Gershwin Godowsky, interview, 7 August 1990

ISAAC GOLDBERG

. . . his parents held no high hopes for his future. He was, frankly, a bad child. He was guilty of petty pilfering; he ran the gamut of minor infractions. With a little less luck he might have become a gangster, for the neighborhood in which his father's first restaurant was situated was also the neighborhood that bred Lefty Louis and Gyp the Blood.

Public school was much of a nuisance, and home work – when it came – drudgery. All that George remembers of school music, which was simply a nuisance within a nuisance, are such ditties as *Annie Laurie* and such belabored classics as *The Lost Chord*. He was especially haunted by the Sullivan song and by the Scotch tune, 'I'll take the high road and you take the low road.' (*Loch Lomond*).

Isaac Goldberg, *George Gershwin* (New York, 1931), pp. 57, 55

HENRY O. OSGOOD
(1879–1927)

A musical journalist–critic, Osgood reported on music in Germany, Italy, France and eventually New York for the *Musical Courier*. He was named its associate editor in 1914 and became one of Gershwin's earliest supporters. While working on a book he interviewed the composer:

'Didn't you play anything when you were a youngster?,' I asked him.
  'Nothing but hookey,' said he.

The peculiar thing is that he has no musical inheritance at all. Neither of his parents knew anything about music, nor, as far as he knows, is there any musical history in generations farther back.

Henry O. Osgood, *So This is Jazz* (Boston, 1926), p. 172

ISAAC GOLDBERG

The child wonder [Max Rosen*] attended the same school that George went to . . . He had played at a school entertainment after the recess for lunch. George had not been interested enough to attend the performance, but the strains of the violin, floating down to him from the assembly hall, had suddenly thrilled him with Dvořák's *Humoresque*.

'It was, to me, a flashing revelation,' [Gershwin recalled] . . . 'I made up my mind to get acquainted with this fellow, and I waited outside from three to four-thirty, in hopes of greeting him. It was pouring cats and dogs, and I got soaked to the skin . . . I found out where he lived and dripping wet as I was, trekked to his house, unceremoniously presenting myself as an admirer . . . Yes, Max opened the world of music to me. And he came near closing it too. When we'd play hooky together, we'd talk eternally about music – that is, when we weren't wrestling. I used to throw him every time, by the way, though he was one of those chubby, stocky kids. He wasn't at all kind to my budding ambitions. And there came a climactic day when he told me flatly that I had better give up all thought of a musical career. "You haven't it in you, Georgie; take my word for it, I can tell!" '

Isaac Goldberg, *George Gershwin* (New York, 1931), pp. 58–9

IRA GERSHWIN

It was when we were living on Second Avenue that my mother added a piano to our home. George was about twelve at the time. No sooner had the upright been lifted through the window to the 'front-room' floor than George sat down and played a popular song of the day. I remember being particularly impressed by his left hand. I had no idea

---

*Rosen (1900–56) studied with Leopold Auer, made his début at fifteen; in his later years he was a respected teacher in New York.

he could play and found out that despite his roller skating activities, the kid parties he attended, the many street games he participated in (with an occasional resultant bloody nose) he had found time to experiment on a player-piano at the home of a friend on Seventh Street. Although the piano was purchased with my taking lessons in mind, it was decided George might prove the brighter pupil. His first teacher was a Miss Green. She was succeeded by a Hungarian band leader, impressively moustached, who was down on his uppers and condescended to take an occasional student. Composer of a *Theodore Roosevelt March*, his fancy ran to band and orchestra literature and George was studying a piano version of the *William Tell* Overture when he was brought to Charles Hambitzer, a talented pianist and composer of light music.

Ira Gershwin, 'My Brother', *George Gershwin*, Merle Armitage, ed. (New York, 1938), p. 17

CHARLES HAMBITZER
(1881–1918)

Pianist, composer, conductor and teacher, he was also a violinist and cellist. He settled in New York in 1908, performed with leading orchestras and became a popular teacher of piano. He composed a couple of operettas and some songs, though these disappeared after his untimely death. Gershwin credited Hambitzer with making him 'harmony-conscious' and introducing him to the works of Chopin, Liszt and Debussy.

I have a pupil who will make his mark in music if anybody will. The boy is a genius, without a doubt; he's just crazy about music and can't wait until it's time to take his lesson. No watching the clock for this boy! He wants to go in for this modern stuff, jazz and what not. But I'm not going to let him for a while. I'll see that he gets a firm foundation in the standard music first.

Charles Hambitzer, from a letter to his sister, Mrs E. Reel (quoted in Goldberg's *George Gershwin*, p. 61)

IRA GERSHWIN

Hambitzer, quick to recognize his ability, encouraged his harmonies and introduced him to the works of the masters, with special emphasis on Chopin and Debussy. George attended the High School of Commerce for a short period [*c*. 1913–14]. During that time he was a pianist for the morning assembly exercises.

Ira Gershwin, 'My Brother', *George Gershwin*, Merle Armitage, ed. (New York, 1938), p. 17

EDWARD KILENYI, SEN.
(1884–1968)

Hungarian-born, he studied with Pietro Mascagni, among others. He settled in New York in 1908, working as a conductor, pianist, and composer, as well as a teacher. Gershwin's piano teacher, Hambitzer, sent him to Kilenyi to study theory, harmony and orchestration. He left New York in 1930 and settled in Hollywood, where he continued teaching and wrote background music for films.

Many a time our lessons consisted of analyzing and discussing classical masterpieces. George understood that he was not to learn 'rules' according to which he himself would have to write music, but instead he would be shown what great composers had written, what devices, styles, traditions – later wrongly called rules – they used. Consequently he enjoyed the contents of our textbook, *The Material Used in Musical Composition*, by Percy Goetschius.

Edward Kilenyi, Sen., *The Gershwin Years*, Edward Jablonski and Lawrence D. Stewart (New York, 1958; 1973), pp. 83–4

IRA GERSHWIN

At the age of fifteen and for a consideration of fifteen dollars a week George became a pianist in the 'professional department' of Jerome H. Remick and Co., publishers of popular music. He was probably the youngest piano pounder ever employed in Tin Pan Alley. He played all day, travelled to nearby cities to accompany the song pluggers, was sent to vaudeville houses to report which acts were using Remick songs, wrote a tune now and then and, whenever he could, attended concerts.

Ira Gershwin, 'My Brother', *George Gershwin*, Merle Armitage, ed. (New York, 1938), p. 17

HENRY O. OSGOOD

The professional department of a popular publishing house is like an extra noisy hour at the psychopathic ward in Bellevue Hospital. Extra noisy, mind you; ordinarily the professional department is much louder and wilder than a hospital . . . All around are cubicles, theoretically sound proof, each with a piano of uncertain vintage and still more uncertain pitch . . . It took more than this bedlam to dissuade George from his love of music. On the contrary, he throve on it and had the good sense to keep right on with the study of good music outside of business hours.

Henry O. Osgood, *So This is Jazz* (Boston, 1926), p. 175

ISAAC GOLDBERG

The café and movie experience was valuable beyond price. In the office and out, Gershwin watched his audiences. He saw what took, and what didn't; he asked himself why. The singers for whom he played the new tunes were, without realizing it, beginning to weary of dull, stereotyped dance patterns. They were wearying too, of sloppy, sirupy melodies. The harmonies had been worn threadbare; they were meaningless, tasteless filler for equally meaningless tunes. The café patrons, he saw, wanted snap and 'pep'; pep, indeed, was just beginning to come into our vocabulary, and by the same token, into our life. And pep was part of George's nature. He had been made for the new day.

Isaac Goldberg, *George Gershwin* (New York, 1931), pp. 75–6

FRED ASTAIRE
(1899–1987)

Born Fred Austerlitz, in his teens he formed a dancing partnership with his sister, Adele (1897–1981). They appeared in vaudeville as a song-and-dance team before the First World War, but scored their first hit in *For Goodness' Sake* in 1922; they were equally successful in London, where the revue was entitled *Stop Flirting*. Their first major New York success was Gershwin's *Lady, be Good!*, after which the Astaires enjoyed a succession of Broadway (and London) successes, until Adele retired after appearing in *The Band Wagon*, becoming Lady Cavendish. Astaire went off to Hollywood where he experienced even greater successes in more than thirty Hollywood musicals, among them some of the finest ever filmed, with such dancing partners as Ginger Rogers, Judy Garland, Rita Hayworth, Jane Powell, even Gene Kelly. His outstanding films include *Top Hat, Shall We Dance, Swing Time, Holiday Inn, Easter Parade, The Band Wagon* and *Funny Face*.

I would go to the various publishers looking for material, and George was a piano player demonstrating songs . . . We struck up a friendship at once. He was amused by my piano playing and often made me play for him. I had a sort of knocked-out slap left hand technique and the beat pleased him. He'd often stop me and say, 'Wait a minute, Freddie, do that one again.'

Fred Astaire, *Steps in Time* (New York, 1959), p. 55

IRA GERSHWIN

One day George submitted a song of his own to the professional manager. He was told: 'You're here as a pianist, not a writer. We've got plenty of writers under contract.' Shortly after, he gave up his job. At this stage he became rehearsal pianist for the Dillingham–Ziegfeld production *Miss 1917*. During a Sunday night 'concert' at the Century Theatre where *Miss 1917* was playing (and the cast had the night off),

Miss Vivienne Segal introduced two of his numbers, 'You-oo, just you' and 'There's more to a kiss than the X-X-X', both with lyrics by Irving Caesar. These brought him to the attention of Max Dreyfus, then head of Harms, Inc., music publishers. He signed with Dreyfus at thirty-five dollars a week. Although he had many more financially flattering offers he decided his place was with Dreyfus, who was not only a publisher of musical comedies and operettas but also a fine musician and student of the classics. During this time he continued his studies with Edward Kilenyi and then Rubin Goldmark.

Ira Gershwin, 'My Brother', *George Gershwin*, Merle Armitage, ed. (New York, 1938), pp. 17–18

II
Discovery

ISAAC GOLDBERG

Gershwin's first printed composition was brought out [in 1916, when he was about seventeen] not by Remick's but by Harry Von Tilzer . . . The words of the first published song – 'When you want 'em, you can't get 'em, when you've got 'em, you don't want 'em' – were written by Murray Roth* who [according to Gershwin] 'got an advance of fifteen dollars for the song. I waived an advance, wanting my royalties' – glamorous word! – 'in a lump sum. After some time I went to Von Tilzer and asked for a little cash for the song. He handed me five dollars. And I never got a cent more from him.' . . .

[Gershwin], without knowing it, must already have decided upon composition as his life work. For, when Irving Berlin, impressed with George's facility at the piano and with his innate feeling for harmony, offered him a position as musical secretary, Gershwin and Berlin, between them, came to the conclusion that George had better not accept . . . Had Gershwin entered upon these duties, the history of American popular music, and not of our popular music alone, would in all likelihood have been radically different . . . Gershwin was determined to remain on his own. To Irving Berlin, too, must go the credit for having discerned in Gershwin, at once, something more than the pounding plugger of Tin Pan Alley.

'You're more than the skilled arranger that I am looking for,' he told Gershwin. 'You're a natural-born creator. This sort of job would cramp you. You're meant for big things.'

Isaac Goldberg, *George Gershwin* (New York, 1931), pp. 85, 90–91

*Roth soon left songwriting and became a Hollywood executive.

IRA GERSHWIN

3 September 1917

Labor Day. With Harry B [Botkin, their artist cousin] to see Rita
Gould at Proctor's 58th Street Theatre. Her accompanist being none
other than George Gershwin alias George Wynne.*

19 October 1917

George continues working at the Century Theatre as rehearsal pianist.
He works quite hard but comes in contact with such notables as Jerome
Kern, Victor Herbert, P. G. Wodehouse, Ned Wayburn, Cecil Lean
and wife, Margot Kelly, Vivienne Segal, Lew Fields et al.

18 December 1917

George sold 'You Just You' to Remick's.

20 January 1918

On Sunday with George . . . to the Majestic Theatre, Brooklyn,
where met Louise Dresser . . . who with George is trying out a new
act.

10 February 1918

George has been placed on the staff of T. B. Harms Co. He gets $35
a week for this connection, then $50 advance and a 3¢ royalty on each
song of his they accept. This entails no other effort on his part than
the composing, they not requiring any of his leisure for plugging nor
for piano-playing. Some snap.

Ira Gershwin, extracts from his *Journal*

ISAAC GOLDBERG

Although *La Lucille* is the first full musical comedy for which Gershwin provided the score, he underwent his baptism of fire several
months earlier with a strange agglomeration christened (perhaps from

---

*Gershwin at this time considered using 'Wynne' as his professional name; around this time
too he used several pseudonyms as a piano-roll recording artist: Bert Wynn, Fred Murtha,
James Baker.

the hour at which it was hoped the curtain would rise) *Half Past Eight*.

Mr [Max] Dreyfus was the patron not only of promising young composers, but also of promising – and sometimes only promissory – producers. So, when an enthusiastic gentleman named Mr [Edward B.] Perkins called with a scheme to produce a revue, Dreyfus not only gave him an advance but offered to pay for the necessary orchestrations. Perkins had brought over some songs and special effects from Paris. He was something of a versifier himself and needed five additional numbers to eke out the production. Could Mr Dreyfus suggest a composer? *Could* he? Why, right in his office he had a clever kid who was just the fellow Perkins was looking for . . . George got the job.

The show was scheduled to open in Syracuse [NY], and when a local organization bought out the first night for $800 it looked as if *Half Past Eight* were to go all around the clock. The entertainment was divided into two parts. The first curtain went up at a quarter to nine and dropped at half past. After an intermission of half an hour the second act opened, running to a 10.45 curtain.

George recalls a single newspaper criticism on the next morning: '*Half Past Eight* isn't even worth the war tax.'

At once uneasiness arose among the cast . . . One of the acts, in fact, mutinied, refusing to go on unless Mr Perkins showed them the color of his money. At the height of the excitement George, in one of his blue suits and with a day's growth of beard, happened to walk backstage. Perkins rushed over to him. 'Listen, George, one of the acts has just refused to go on. You'll have to take their place. It's absolutely necessary; we need the time to make a change of scene.'

George, as is his wont, refused to get excited. 'All right,' he answered, 'but what am I to do?'

'Play some of your hits!' exclaimed Perkins. Hits! Where were they? George would have liked nothing better than to have a medley of hits . . . On the spur of the moment he improvised a melange of his various compositions. Then he arose and walked off. The audience received the offering in gaping puzzlement and George entered the wings to the accompaniment of a cast silence. Not a hand!

This was not his only emergency contribution to the brief fortunes of *Half Past Eight*. The show had been advertised as sporting a Broadway chorus, which, in reality, had its sole existence in print and in Perkins' imagination. But what was the finale of a revue without a choric ensemble? Whereupon kid Gershwin, in all the astuteness of his nineteen and a half years, gave birth to a brilliant suggestion. Why not, for the finale, send out all the comedians dressed in Chinese pajamas, holding large umbrellas before their faces so as to conceal their sex? 'Ah, here's the chorus!' the audience would exclaim, and perhaps hold their seats till the ordeal was over. The suggestion was eagerly seized upon by Perkins. But how was George to know that the economical producer would procure cheap paper umbrellas? On opening night, three of the umbrellas failed to open, and Syracuse learned too late that men betray.

George managed to get his fare back to New York. *Half Past Eight* kept dying until Friday night, when it folded its umbrellas and silently stole away.

One solace the thwarted composer carried back home with him: he had seen, at last, on a billboard, the proclamative legend, 'Music by George Gershwin.'

Isaac Goldberg, *George Gershwin* (New York, 1931), pp. 95–8

IRVING CAESAR

(b. 1895)

Lyricist and composer, following graduation from the City College of New York, he served as a stenographer to Henry Ford's Peace Ship. Although he studied piano as a child, he drifted into Tin Pan Alley and began writing lyrics for revues and shows, making his mark with Gershwin in 'Swanee'. Among Caesar's collaborators were Vincent Youmans (*No, No, Nanette*: 'Tea for two'), Rudolph Friml, Oscar Levant and Sigmund Romberg.

We were walking down Broadway and there was a song that was a very big hit at the time, 'Hindustan', a one-step. I said to George, 'Why don't we write an American one-step, why does it have to be Hindustan?' We wrote 'Swanee' in ten minutes – ten minutes!

Irving Caesar, interview, *American Masters: George Gershwin*, Public Broadcasting System, 24 August 1987

That evening we had dinner at Dinty Moore's, discussed the song, boarded a Riverside Drive bus, got up to his home on Washington Heights, and immediately went to the piano alcove, separated by the inevitable beaded curtain of the period from the dining room. There was a poker game in progress at the time. In about fifteen minutes we had turned out 'Swanee', verse and chorus. But we thought the song should have a trio and for a few minutes we were deciding about this addition. The losers in the game kept saying, 'Boys, finish it some other time' and the lucky ones urged us to complete the song then and there. This we did, and old man Gershwin lost not a moment in fetching a comb, over which he superimposed some tissue, and accompanying George while I sang it over and over again at the insistence of the winning poker players.

Irving Caesar, *The Gershwin Years*, Edward Jablonski and Lawrence D. Stewart (New York 1958; 1973), p. 67

ISAAC GOLDBERG

Some nine months after the song was written, Al Jolson happened to be appearing in *Sinbad*. He heard the song (Gershwin played it at a party). He guessed at hidden possibilities and adopted it then and there for his spectacle.

The rest is history in Racket Tow. A failure (in the *Capitol Revue*) was turned, overnight, into a phenomenal success. The song spread like wildfire, from coast to coast, from border to border. The phonograph recording alone sold 2,250,000 copies. Two years later it was still the rage of the season in London. What had done it? It is hard to say. It is not one of Gershwin's best tunes; but it had an invigorating rhythm that simply woke the potentialities of the national popular song to new life.

George Gershwin was made.

Isaac Goldberg, *George Gershwin* (New York, 1931), p. 99

IRA GERSHWIN

Beginning in 1920 [George] wrote among other things, the music for *George White's Scandals* for five consecutive years. It was for the third of this series that he and B. G. DeSylva turned out in six days a short one-act opera called *135th Street*.*

Ira Gershwin, 'My Brother', *George Gershwin*, Merle Armitage, ed. (New York, 1938), p. 19

ISAAC GOLDBERG

Buddy DeSylva, one of the cleverest lyricists that ever forced a rhyme in Tin Pan Alley . . . in the early 1920s was discussing with Gershwin the possibilities of an opera . . . It was the hey-day of the new jazz, and Gotham was in the midst of a concurrent Negrophilia. Together they brought this black idea to the producer, George White. At once, he saw its possibilities . . . On second thought, White suggested that DeSylva and Gershwin hold back for a while. [As all performers in the *Scandals* were white, he visualized make-up problems between acts.] Nevertheless, three weeks before the show opened he came to the collaborators and announced that he would like to have a try at the experiment anyway . . . For five days and nights they toiled on this pioneer one-act vaudeville opera and on the sixth they arose and found it good.

George was keyed to high pitch. The opening night was a tremendous tax on his nerves. From this occasion, indeed, he dates his famous nervous indigestion.

The opera – in New Haven – went over magnificently. 'This opera,' wrote one critic, 'will be imitated in a hundred years.' . . . *Blue Monday Blues* [*sic*] received scant notice in the New York press on the morning after the night before.†

Charles Darton, in the *World*, was short and sour, and must have given the collaborators another case of blue Monday blues. The piece, he found, was '. . . the most dismal, stupid and incredible blackface sketch that has probably ever been perpetrated. In it a dusky soprano finally killed her gambling man. She should have shot all her associates the moment they appeared and then turned the pistol on herself.'

*The title of the work was initially *Blue Monday*: when Paul Whiteman revived it in 1925 for a Carnegie Hall concert, with a new orchestration by Ferde Grofé, it was retitled *135th Street*.

†*Blue Monday* was performed for one night, on 28 August 1922. Paul Whiteman presented it at his second 'Experiment' at Carnegie Hall on 29 December 1925 and 1 January 1926.

Some reviewers did not mention *Blue Monday* at all, but there was
a positive, prescient opinion from one, modestly signing his opinion
with his initials, 'W.S.'.

*Although Mr White or any of his confrers may not be aware of it, they
will have done a thing which will, or ought to, go down in history; they
have given us the first real American opera . . . Here at last is a genuinely
human plot of American life, set to music in the popular vein, using jazz
only at the right moments, the sentimental song, the Blues, and above all,
a new and free ragtime recitative. True, there were crudities, but in it we
see the first gleam of a new American musical art.*

Isaac Goldberg, *George Gershwin* (New York, 1931), pp. 120–23

CARL VAN VECHTEN
(1880–1964)

Author, critic and photographer, Carl Van Vechten wrote
music and dance criticism for the *New York Times*; by the
1920s he was a major figure in New York's cultural life,
with a flair for contemporary musicians (he was the first
to write about Stravinsky and Gershwin, among others),
popular arts (Broadway songs, jazz, film) and black artists.
A novelist, he published the ground-breaking *Nigger
Heaven* in 1926 and the scholarly but fascinating *The Tiger
in the House* in 1920. He founded the George Gershwin
Memorial Collection of Music and Musical Literature at
Fisk University, Nashville, Tennessee. He and Gershwin
discussed collaboration on an opera, but it never came off.
The recipient of the letter quoted below is identified only
as 'a newspaper friend' by Gershwin's biographer Isaac
Goldberg.

I've just had some good news . . . Eva Gauthier telephoned me last
night that on the program of her first concert to be given early in
November she will put a jazz group. She is doing this great service
to the American people in no half-hearted way, either; the songs are
not to be sandwiched in between opera airs and English ballads. They
are immediately preceded in the program by the name of Béla Bartók,

and they are followed by selections from Schoenberg's *Gurrelieder*! George Gershwin is to play her accompaniments for this group, which will include his splendid 'I'll build a stairway to paradise' . . . I consider this one of the very most important events in American musical history.

Carl Van Vechten, quoted by Isaac Goldberg, *George Gershwin* (New York, 1931), pp. 126–7

In the spring of 1923, Eva Gauthier, indefatigable in her search for novelties, asked me to suggest additions to her autumn program. 'Why not a group of American songs?' I urged. Her face betrayed her lack of interest. 'Jazz,' I particularized. Her expression brightened. Meeting this singer again in September, on her return from Paris, she informed me that Ravel had offered her the same sapient advice. She had, indeed, determined to adopt the idea and requested me to recommend a musician who might serve as her accompanist in this venture. But one name fell from my lips, that of George Gershwin . . . The experiment was eventually made . . . given at Town Hall on November 1, 1923, [it] marked George Gershwin's initial appearance as a performer on the serious concert stage.

Carl Van Vechten, *Vanity Fair*, March 1925, p. 40

EVA GAUTHIER

(1885–1958)

> A Canadian-born mezzo-soprano who began to study music as a child in a convent, Eva Gauthier studied further in London, Paris and Rome. Beginning in 1910 she toured the Orient and then settled in New York, where she became an advocate of such contemporaries as Schoenberg, Stravinsky and Bartók, and young Americans, among them Charles T. Griffes and, in time, Gershwin. After retirement from singing, she taught in New York.

Now let me go back fourteen years – such a short time ago – and quote from the *Literary Digest* of November 24, 1923, a summary of a review by Deems Taylor of a New York concert at Aeolian Hall, November 1, 1923, at which George Gershwin accompanied me in a group of songs of his own composition, and others by Irving Berlin, Jerome Kern and Walter Donaldson. 'A pause,' [Taylor wrote]. 'The singer reappeared, followed by a tall, black-haired young man who was far from possessing the icy aplomb of those to whom playing on the platform of Aeolian Hall is an old story. He bore under his arm a small bundle of sheet music with lurid black and red and yellow covers. The audience began to show signs of relaxation; this promised to be amusing . . . Young Mr Gershwin began to do mysterious and fascinating rhythmic and contrapuntal stunts with the accompaniment . . . by the time "Swanee" arrived he [a "distinguished European" musician Taylor did not identify] was having as shamelessly good a time as anybody.'

Eva Gauthier, *George Gershwin*, Merle Armitage, ed. (New York, 1938), pp. 193–4

HENRY TAYLOR PARKER
(1867–1934)

A critic and author, after graduating from Harvard, Henry Taylor Parker joined the staff of the Boston *Evening Transcript* as its New York correspondent; he later did the same in London. He returned to become the paper's leading drama and music critic (though he could not read music), a post he held until his death. His review of the Gauthier Boston recital follows.

[Gershwin's playing improved] the jazz songs . . . He diversified them with cross-rhythms; wove them into pliant and outspringing counterpoint; set in pauses and accents; sustained cadences; gave character to the measures wherein the singer's voice was still . . . He reins or looses sentiment as in 'Swanee' with a discriminating will. Humor tempts him in [innocent] 'Ingenue baby' and 'Do it again'. With accent and color he is making conscious strokes of the theatre as he builds the Stairway to Paradise. From him the Europeans – Casella,

Milhaud and others – might draw hints and profits. In America, and above Mr Berlin, he is the beginning of the age of sophisticated jazz.

'H.T.P.', Boston *Evening Transcript*, 30 January 1924

III
Rhapsody in Blue

IRA GERSHWIN

The newspaper item was the first inkling George had that Whiteman was serious when he had once casually mentioned that some day he expected to do such a concert and hoped for a contribution from George. Finding in his notebooks a theme (the clarinet glissando) which he thought might make an appropriate opening for a more extended work than he had been accustomed to writing, he decided to chance it.

Ira Gershwin, 'My Brother', *George Gershwin*, Merle Armitage, ed. (New York, 1938), p. 20

HENRY O. OSGOOD

George Gershwin, a pianist both rapid and rabid, responded by writing a piece for himself and jazz orchestra, and his lieutenant, Ferdie Grofe [*sic*], confronted with an entirely new problem in orchestration, solved it with ingenuity and promptness. The whole job was completed in ten days.

Henry O. Osgood, 'The Jazz Bugaboo', *American Mercury*, November 1925

FERDE GROFÉ
(1892–1972)

> At the time, Ferde Grofé was Whiteman's chief arranger and pianist. He eventually left Whiteman to lead his own orchestra and to write. His own compositions include *Grand Canyon Suite*, *Mississippi Suite* and *Three Shades of Blue*.

I orchestrated the *Rhapsody* from the composer's sketch for two pianos . . . He lived with his parents and brothers and sister, all of

them children, except Ira, and I practically lived too at their uptown
Amsterdam Avenue and 110th Street apartment, for I called daily for
more pages of George's masterpiece . . . He and his brother Ira had
a back room where there was an upright piano, and that is where the
Rhapsody grew into being. During that time I learned to value the
atmosphere of George's home, and the sweet hospitality of his mother
and father. Mrs Gershwin watched our labors with loving interest,
and taught me to appreciate Russian tea, which she brewed for us
when we rested.

Ferde Grofé, *George Gershwin*, Merle Armitage, ed. (New York, 1938),
p. 28

PAUL WHITEMAN
(1890–1967)

From a distinguished musical family, Paul Whiteman
began his musical career as violinist and violist in the
Denver Symphony, and later in the San Francisco Symphony. During World War I he played in the US Navy
band. In 1919 he formed a dance band that was so popular
on the West Coast that he was invited to New York, where
he began recording and performing to become one of the
most successful bands of the 1920s in the US and Europe.
The Whiteman band featured written arrangements based
on the music of black jazz music. His 1924 'Experiment
in Modern Music' initiated a rash of 'symphonic jazz'.
Whiteman tried, but never equalled that event – though
he remained a popular radio (and later, television) figure
into the mid-1950s.

Fifteen minutes before the concert was to begin, I yielded to a nervous
longing to see for myself what was happening out front, and putting
on an overcoat over my concert clothes, I slipped around to the entrance
of Aeolian Hall.

There I gazed upon a picture that should have imparted new vigor
to my wilting confidence. It was snowing, but men and women were
fighting to get in the door . . . Such was my state of mind by this
time, that I wondered if I had come to the right entrance. And then

I saw Victor Herbert [who had contributed *A Suite of Serenades* to the concert] going in. It was the right entrance, sure enough, and the next day, the ticket office people said they could have sold out the house ten times over.

I went back stage again, more scared than ever. Black fear simply possessed me. I paced the floor, gnawed my thumbs and vowed I'd give $5,000 if I could stop right then and there . . . But never in my life had I such stage fright as that day.

Paul Whiteman and Mary Margaret McBride, *Jazz* (New York, 1926), pp. 97–8

OLIN DOWNES

(1886–1955)

Author and, at the time, music critic for the *New York Times*.

The stage setting was as unconventional as the program. Pianos in various stages of undress stood about, amid a litter of every imaginable contraption of wind and percussion instruments. Two Chinese mandarins, surmounting pillars, looked down upon a scene that would have curdled the blood of a Stokowski or a Mengelberg. The golden sheen of the brass instruments of lesser or greater dimensions was caught up by the Chinese gong and carried out by bright patches of an Oriental back-drop. There were also lying or hanging about frying pans, large tin utensils and a speaking trumpet, later stuck into the end of a trombone – and what a silky tone came from that accommodating instrument! This singular assemblage of things was more than once, in some strange way, to combine to evoke fascinating and beautiful sonorities. It was – should we blush to say it? – a phase of America. It reminded the writer of someone's remark that an Englishman entered a place as if he were its master, whereas an American entered as if he didn't care who in blazes the master might be. Something like that was in the music. Then stepped on the stage, sheepishly, a lank and dark young man – George Gershwin.

. . . the audience was stirred, and many a hardened concertgoer excited with the sensation of finding a new talent finding its voice and likely to say something important personally and racially to the world.

Olin Downes, *New York Times*, 13 February 1924

THE CRITICS

The reception of the Whiteman 'Experiment' was unusual in that the reviews tended to concentrate on Gershwin's contribution. They were, in a word, mixed. All of the critics were ignorant of the definition of the word 'jazz', and most had never experienced such sounds before. Some – Gabriel and Taylor – were delighted, and others – such as Gilman – were repelled. This established the pattern of Gershwin's future judgement by the 'serious' critics through to his final major work, *Porgy and Bess*. He enjoyed good reviews, but so far as is known, he was never particularly bothered by negative appraisals of his work; he was already on to the next project.

To begin with, Mr Whiteman's experiment was an uproarious success. This music conspicuously possesses superb vitality and ingenuity of rhythm, mastery of novel and beautiful effects of timbre. For Jazz is basically a kind of rhythm plus a kind of instrumentation. But it seems to us that this music is only half alive. Its gorgeous vitality of rhythm and of instrumental color is impaired by melodic and harmonic anemia of the most pernicious kind . . . Recall the most ambitious piece, the *Rhapsody*, and weep over the lifelessness of its melody and harmony, so derivative, so stale, so inexpressive. And then recall for contrast, the rich inventiveness of the rhythms, the saliency and vividness of the orchestral color.

Lawrence Gilman, *New York Tribune*, 13 February 1924

Mr Gershwin's composition proved to be a highly ingenious work, treating the piano in a manner calling for much technical skill and furnishing an orchestral background in which saxophones, trombones and clarinets are merged in a really skillful piece of orchestration. If this way lies the path toward the development of American modern music into a high art form, then one can heartily congratulate Mr Gershwin on his disclosure of some of the possibilities.

W. J. Henderson, *New York Herald*, 13 February 1924

The title rhapsody was a just one for Mr Gershwin's composition suitable to covering a degree of formlessness to which the middle section of the work, relying too steadily on tort and retort of the piano, seemed to lag. But the beginning and ending of it were stunning. The beginning particularly, with a flutter-tongued, drunken whoop of an introduction that had the audience rocking. Mr Gershwin has an irrepressible pack of talents.

Gilbert Gabriel, *New York Sun*, 13 February 1924

Mr Gershwin will be heard from often, and one music lover who became an admirer of his art last Tuesday afternoon earnestly hopes that he will keep to the field in which he is a free and independent creator, and not permit himself to be led away into the academic groves and buried in the shadows of ancient trees.

W. J. Henderson, *New York Herald*, 17 February 1924

[The *Rhapsody in Blue*] shows extraordinary talent, just as it also shows a young composer with aims that go far beyond those of his ilk, struggling with a form of which he is far from being master . . . Often Mr Gershwin's purpose is defeated by technical immaturity, but in spite of that . . . he has expressed himself in a significant, and on the whole, highly original manner. His first theme alone, with its caprice, humor and exotic outline, shows a talent to be reckoned with . . . It is an idea, or several ideas correlated and combined, in varying and well-contrasted rhythms that immediately intrigue the hearer. This, in essence, is fresh and new, full of future promise . . . The second theme, with a lovely sentimental line, is more after the manner of some of Mr Gershwin's colleagues. The tuttis are too long, cadenzas are too long. The peroration at the end loses a large measure of wildness and magnificence it easily could have if it were more broadly prepared.

Olin Downes, *New York Times*, 13 February 1924

[Whiteman and Gershwin] have added a new chapter to our musical history.

Henrietta Strauss, *The Nation*, 5 March 1924

CARL VAN VECHTEN

The concert, quite as a matter of course, was a riot; you crowned it with, after repeated hearings, I am forced to regard as the foremost serious effort by an American composer. Go straight on and you will knock all Europe silly. Go a little farther in the next one and invent a new *form*. I think something might be done in the way of combining jazz and the moving-picture technique. Think of the themes as close-ups, flashbacks, etc.! This is merely an impertinent suggestion; what-ever you do, however, including playing the piano, you do so well that you need no advice.

Marguerite d'Alvarez,* by the way, was reduced to a state of hysterical enthusiasm by the concert, especially your contribution. She wants to sing at the next one! You might tell Whiteman this: she would certainly give the audience a good time.

Carl Van Vechten, letter to George Gershwin, 14 February 1924

*Billed as a 'Peruvian contralto' (though born in Liverpool), she, like Eva Gauthier, would join Gershwin on the recital stage. For a series of concerts beginning on 5 December 1926, he composed his piano preludes and accompanied her in a group of his songs. The programme lists five preludes (later there were six), of which three were published.

IV

'. . . A Young Colossus . . .'

The impact of the *Rhapsody in Blue* on the American musical scene was immediate and dramatic: critics argued over the merits and the meretriciousness of what they called 'jazz'. (Actually it was popular song and dance ingeniously arranged; Paul Whiteman's standard orchestra was not a jazz band, though it was probably one of the earliest harbingers of the 'big bands' that would flourish in the later thirties.) Because of his association with jazz, Gershwin too came under fire as a kind of Tin Pan Alley upstart who slipped into Carnegie Hall via Broadway. He was interviewed and written about, and began early in 1924 to live a very public life; and he loved it. He was sought after for elegant, fashionable parties where he was expected to play – and he did, for hours. After his *Rhapsody*, in Isaac Goldberg's rather breathless phrase about Gershwin: 'With one foot just outside Tin Pan Alley and the other planted on Carnegie Hall he bestrode the musical world of Gotham like a young Colossus.' He was, at twenty-five, *the* George Gershwin. On 18 November 1924, shortly before the opening of his first major musical comedy success, *Lady, be Good!*, he was mentioned in the *New York Times* in company with the two men he admired most, Irving Berlin and Jerome Kern. In this article musical patron Otto Kahn had discussed the possibility of producing an 'American jazz opera' at the Metropolitan and his intention of talking to these three musical giants: only Gershwin finally made it – six decades after his death.

CARL VAN VECHTEN*

I wrote a paper, entitled *The Great American Composer*, published in *Vanity Fair* for April 1917, in which I outlined the reasons for my belief that it was out of American popular music that American art music would grow, just as . . . so much European art music has evolved from national folksong. Nearly seven years have passed before my prophecy was realized, but on February 12, 1924, a date which many of us will remember henceforth as commemorative of another event of importance besides the birth of our most famous president, George Gershwin's *Rhapsody in Blue* was performed for the first time by Paul Whiteman's Orchestra with the composer at the piano . . . I never entertained a single doubt that this young man of twenty-five . . . had written the finest piece of serious music that had ever come out of America; moreover, that he had composed the most effective concerto for piano that anybody had written since Tchaikovsky's B flat minor.

Enthusiasm rewarded the first performance of the *Rhapsody*, but general and adequate appreciation of the glamor and vitality of the composition, exhibiting, as it does, a puissant melodic gift in combination with a talent for the invention of striking rhythms and a felicity in the arrangement of form, did not come so rapidly, perhaps, as a ready admiration for the composer's obviously rare skill as pianist. After Gershwin had performed the concerto several times in New York and other cities (Whiteman undertook a preliminary tour with his organization during the spring of 1924), recognition of its superior qualities became more widely diffused; the abridged phonograph disc (even both sides of a twelve-inch disc offer insufficient surface to record the piece in its entirety) added to its fame; and the publication of the score, arranged for two pianos, in December, sealed its triumph. It has since been performed, although seldom with the composer at the piano, at nearly every concert given by the Whiteman Orchestra. Two causes have interfered with more general performances: first, the fact that the work is scored for a jazz band; second, the fact that the piano part is not only of transcendent difficulty but also demands a

---

*Van Vechten took great pride in being the first to write a lengthy and serious article on Gershwin for a major publication.

pianist who understands the spirit of jazz. I have no doubt whatever but that so soon as an arrangement is made for symphony orchestra the *Rhapsody* will become a part of the repertory of any pianist who can play it. Quite possibly, the work may have its flaws; so, on the other hand, has *Tristan und Isolde*.

Carl Van Vechten, 'George Gershwin, An American Composer who is Writing Notable Music in the Jazz Idiom', *Vanity Fair*, March 1925

FRANKLIN PIERCE ADAMS
(1881–1960)

A journalist and author who was known professionally as 'F.P.A.', Franklin Pierce Adams began as a newspaper columnist with the *Chicago Journal*, then continued in New York on the *Evening World*, *Tribune*, *World*, *Herald-Tribune*, etc. His 'Conning Tower' weekly column consisted of quips, light verse, often contributions from such writer friends as Dorothy Parker and Ring Lardner. His Saturday column in the style of Samuel Pepys covered New York's art, music, theatre and party world of the 1920s. In 1909 Adams collaborated with writer O. Henry on a musical comedy, *Lo!* (music by A. Baldwin Sloane, lyrics by Adams), a classic failure. He never tried this kind of writing again.

Saturday 24 January 1926

George Gershwin the composer came in, and we did talk about musique, and about going ahead regardless of advice, this one saying, Do not study, and that one saying, Study; and another saying, Write only jazz melodies, and another saying, Write only symphonies and concertos. But the thing to do is what you want to do, for all advice is of no moment.

Sunday 7 February 1926

W. Cox and Dot Knight to dinner, and in the evening G. Gershwin and Will Daly came in, and played G.'s *Concerto* and his *Rhapsody in Blue*; and I never did enjoy musique more in my life.

Sunday, 14 February 1926

Up be times, and at this and that task all the day, and in the evening
E. Zimbalist and Alma [Gluck, his wife, the noted soprano] and Alice
Kindler [wife of Hans Kindler, a cellist] and F. Crowninshield [editor
of *Vanity Fair*] to dinner, and so all to G. Gershwin's, to a great party
and a deal of musique, and some anticks, but what I enjoyed more
than aught ever I heard were some songs sung by [the songwriting
team of] Bert Kalmar and Harry Ruby, one after another, and none
so merry as a patriotick song called 'America, I love you'.

Tuesday 26 May 1926

So home, and fell to work till past 10 o'clock, with great zest, too,
and then come Will Daly and G. Gershwin and A. Huxley and his
wife, too; and George and Will did play some of George's works,
such as his Concerto and his *Rhapsody in Blue*, which delighted Mr
and Mrs H. greatly, and which I do like better each time I hear it.
Lord!

Tuesday 9 November 1926

So home, and with my wife to see *Oh, Kay!* a pleasant harlequinade
with musick. I like the best of all G. Gershwin's [music], and Miss
[Gertrude] Lawrence full of grace and merry fragility.

Monday 6 December 1926

So to the Plymouth Theatre with G. Gershwin, to see 'The Pirates of
Penzance', brimming with melody and sweet lyrics.

Sunday 19 June 1927

So played at croquet all afternoon, with G. and I. Gershwin, and my
partner was Will Daly, and we did well enough, winning and losing,
and doing the best when H. [lyricist Howard] Dietz was one of our
opponents. So listened in the evening to G. Gershwin's playing of
some newly written pieces,* highly enjoyable, and thence home.

Sunday 15 December 1929

So after dinner uptown to G. Gershwin's, and there to was a marionette
show given, a thing written and directed by young John Huston. It
was a dramatization, as you might say, of 'Frankie and Johnny', and
it was not the way I thought it would be at all, forasmuch as the

---

*According to F. P. A., this was the score for *Strike up the Band*.

characters were vocal, and the play was done in prose for the most part. And it was as beautiful a thing as I ever saw, and wrote with a skill and lyrickall sense that I thought exceptional.

Sunday 22 October 1933

Up of a warm Sunday morning that made me wish I were in the country, and so worked at some writing, and in the afternoon to meet G. [newspaper writer Geoffrey] Parsons at the tennis court, and he beat me, but he and I beat two young fellows that invited us to play, one of the lads being George Gershwin, and so home to supper.

Franklin P. Adams, *The Diary of our Own Samuel Pepys: 1911–1934* (New York, 1935), pp. 501, 507, 585, 590, 591–2, 623–4, 673, 683, 734, 921–2, 1180

HENRY O. OSGOOD*

. . . various composers who deserve serious consideration have written about a dozen or fifteen compositions purporting to the higher jazz and scored for jazz orchestra . . . none of them promises to attain any degree of permanency on concert programs. This leaves, up to the present time, only the Gershwin works, the *Rhapsody in Blue* and the Piano Concerto in F, as representative of a successful attempt to graft upon the great trunk of legitimate music little offshoots of that vigorous sapling which is the only really original thing America has produced in music – Jazz.

. . . he gave us something really new in music. Not more than a dozen composers out of the hundreds on the honor list since the art of composing began have succeeded in doing that.

Henry O. Osgood, *So This is Jazz* (Boston, 1926), pp. 181, 203

*Osgood believed that his book was 'the first attempt to set down a connected account of the origin, history and development of jazz music'. It was not, but it was Gershwin's first serious appraisal in a book – two chapters, in fact, were devoted to his biography and his two larger works.

BEVERLY NICHOLS
(1898–1983)

An Oxford graduate, Beverly Nichols wrote drama criticism for the *Weekly Dispatch*, contributed music to revues
such as *Picnic* (1927), *Cochran's Revue of 1930*, and was the
author of several books including *Crazy Pavements, Prelude, For Adults Only*, and *Self*. He contributed articles
and reviews to the *Sun-Chronicle* and the *Daily Sketch* (in
which his Gershwin interview was originally published).

I am going to begin right in the middle, because until I have made
George Gershwin play you his first piano concerto you will probably
regard him (as do most of our half-baked critics) as a mere pedler of
common tunes, like his 'Swanee', and 'Lady be Good!'. So you must
imagine a swarthy young man of twenty-seven* seated at a piano by
the open window of a room in Pall Mall not long ago, lifting his
fingers and beginning to play. The twilight was fast fading when he
sat down, and by the time he had finished it was almost dark, and the
street lamps were lit. Yet in that brief period I had passed through
one of the most singular musical experiences I have ever known.

I ought to be slightly drunk to be able to describe it properly, for
it was the music of intoxication. Only by ragged words, by a mass of
stage effects, by strident and jagged adjectives could one capture on
the printed page the entangled and enticing rhythms which floated
across the darkening room.

How can I describe those rhythms? Everybody is acquainted, of
course, with the ordinary jazz tricks. Most of them consist in making
a tune hiccup, by a judicious administration of quavers, at the beginning of a bar. Or else, a simple phrase of six quavers, demanding a
three-four tempo, is put into a strait-waistcoat of common time, and
made to wriggle about with most entertaining antics. Everybody knows
these little devices. They are as old as Bach, and probably older. I
realized in the first five minutes that Gershwin was going far beyond
that in his concerto. It would need a very complicated series of math-

---

*The article dated from 1926, when Gershwin was in London for the English production
of his 1924 success, *Lady, be Good*! Starring Fred and Adele Astaire, it opened at the
Empire Theatre, 14 April 1926, and was a hit.

ematical charts to explain exactly what he *was* doing; and even when one had explained it, the number of people who could play the result would, I imagine, be not greater than those who, according to Mr Einstein, comprehended the theory of relativity. To put it in a non-technical way, he was taking a quantity of strictly opposed rhythms and, by some magic counterpoint of his own, weaving them into a glittering mass which was at once as well ordered as a route march and as drunken as an orgy.

Yet beautiful. *Really* beautiful. The visions that this concerto called up before me! I loathe people who make pictures out of music, who grin vacuously and refer to waterfalls when they hear a Liszt cadenza, who poignantly recall their first seduction when listening to a sentimental waltz by Chaminade, and to whom the Preludes of Chopin mean nothing more than rain dripping on a roof or George Sand having the vapours. The world is full of such people, and I have always flattered myself that I was not of their number. Apparently I was mistaken.

For as I listened it seemed that the whole of new America was blossoming into beauty before me. The phrases swept up the piano with the stern, unfaltering grace of a skyscraper. Ever and anon the bass would take into its head to go mad . . . There were passages vivid and humorous – a sort of chattering of Broadway chorus girls drinking mint julep at Child's. There were slow secretive melodies that had in them something of the mystery of vast forests. The tunes clashed and fought, degenerated, were made clean again, joined together, and scampered madly over the keyboard in a final rush which was as breathless as the thundering herd over the prairies of the West.

When it was all over, and the aftermath of silence had gradually been penetrated by the noises of everyday life from the streets outside, I felt that the occasion was one for repeating what Schumann said after hearing Chopin for the first time: 'Hats off gentlemen – a genius.' Only there were no hats to take off, and we should be embarrassed by so un-English a display of emotion. I therefore turned to one of the most complicated pages and asked him, quite bluntly, how it was done.

'I don't know.'

'Please play this bit very slowly.'

He played it. There were three distinct rhythms fighting each other – two in the treble and one in the bass. I began to laugh.

'What are you laughing at?'

'All those rhythms – scrapping. How *do* you make them fight like that?'

He shook his head and went on playing.

'I feel things inside, and then I work them out – that's all.'

'You must have felt pretty volcanic when you wrote this. Do you always feel volcanic?'

'No. An ordinary jazz tune's different.'

While he had been talking, he had been occasionally dabbing at the keyboard with his right hand. Little bits of tunes were born, floated away, died. Now and then he would play a phrase twice, three times, and then smother it with a discord, as though he did not wish to claim its paternity. Then, suddenly, a rather fascinating phrase came out.

'I say,' I said, 'I rather like that.'

'So do I.' He played it again, improvising a 'following' theme. 'It's got possibilities. But it's really a Charleston* tune and it hasn't got a Charleston rhythm.' At which he proceeded to maltreat the poor tune as few tunes have been maltreated. Over and over again he played it, until I felt that I never wanted to hear it again. Then, when it seemed perfect, he said: 'Well, at any rate, that's the beginning.' There – I am writing on silent paper, which has no power of harmony or discord, and I will cease from these descriptions of an art which cannot be described.

Beverly Nichols, *Are They the Same at Home?* (New York, 1927), pp. 108–111

---

*Probably 'I'd rather Charleston', which was interpolated into the London production of *Lady, be Good!* The lyric was by the English lyricist Desmond Carter, and sung as a duet by the Astaires.

RING LARDNER
(1885–1933)
AND
GEORGE S. KAUFMAN
(1889–1961)

Both Lardner and Kaufman were leading satirist-humorists in the twenties and into the thirties. Kaufman worked with the Gershwins on *Strike up the Band* (1927), the Pulitzer prize-winning *Of Thee I Sing* and its sequel, *Let 'em Eat Cake*. For Gershwin to have been an unseen but impressive presence – he virtually empties the stage – was an acknowledgement of his celebrity only six years after *Rhapsody in Blue*.

The scene is a room at Goebel's music publishing house. A piano, a few chairs, some shelves, and you have it . . . Goldie enters.

GOLDIE: Beg pardon, Mr Hart!

HART: Now what?

GOLDIE: George Gershwin's out there.

HART: George Gershwin!

GOLDIE: Yes, sir.

HART: My God! (*He hurries out.*)

FRED: Who is it?

WINDOW CLEANER: George Gershwin (*He also hurries out.*)

BRAINARD: Yeah!

 (BRAINARD, *after a second's hesitation, also goes, hurrying a little.* BENNY *is next to go.*)

PAUL: (*to* FRED) Did you ever see him?

FRED: No.

PAUL: He stole my rhapsody.

 (*He and* FRED *go.*)

Ring Lardner and George S. Kaufman, *June Moon*, Act II (New York, 1930), pp. 113–14

ALEXANDER WOOLLCOTT

(1887–1943)

Drama critic, journalist, radio personality and essayist,
noted equally for his cruel wit and sugary sentimentality.
He wrote for the *New York Times*, the *Herald* and *The
New Yorker*. He was the inspiration for the wasp-tongued
protagonist in the Kaufman and Hart comedy *The Man
Who Came to Dinner*, and appeared in it as himself with
a touring company. Collections of his writings, including
book reviews, short stories, etc. (*While Rome Burns*, 1934,
and *Long, Long Ago*, 1943) were best-sellers.

The first time I ever met George Gershwin, he came to dine with me
at my hotel in Atlantic City. I saw before me a slim, swarthy, brilliant
young man who, with his dark cheeks that could flood with color, his
flashing smile and his marked personal radiance, did, when serving
at the altar we call a piano, achieve a dazzling incandescence. But this
was a mere dinner table, and his fires were banked, his light curtained
in melancholy. He began by apologizing for the eccentric dinner he
would have to order. 'You see,' he explained, 'I have terrible trouble
with my stomach.'

Later I heard a great deal about Gershwin's stomach, and learned
to understand its proper place in this thumb-nail sketch. Like you and
me, Master Gershwin was profoundly interested in himself, but unlike
most of us he had no habit of pretense. He was beyond, and, to my
notion, above, posing. He said exactly what he thought, without
window dressing it to make an impression, favorable or otherwise.
Any salient description of him must begin with this trait. All the
stories told about him derive from it.

When shortly after the French and Indian Wars, I was an under-
graduate at Hamilton College, I introduced to a snowbound group in
the dormitory one afternoon the game of choosing for each person in
our class the one adjective which fitted him more perfectly than any
other. I even ventured the dogmatic assertion that, if we made our
selections well, someone should be able to identify the men from the
list of adjectives . . . Well, if I were thus rationed in this article and

could have but one adjective for George Gershwin, that adjective would be 'ingenuous'.

Ingenuous at and about his piano. Once an occasional composer named Oscar Levant stood beside that piano while those sure, sinewy, catlike Gershwin fingers beat their brilliant drum-fire – the tumultuous cascade of the *Rhapsody in Blue*, the amorous langour of 'The man I love', the impish glee of 'Fascinating Rhythm', the fine jaunty, dust-spurning scorn of 'Strike up the Band'. If the performer was familiar with the work of any other composer, he gave no evidence of it. Levant . . . could be heard muttering under his breath, 'An evening with Gershwin is a Gershwin evening.'

'I wonder', said our young composer dreamily, 'if my music will be played a hundred years from now.'

'It certainly will be,' said the bitter Levant,* 'if you are still around.'

Now all musicians like to be asked to perform, but tradition bids them to do so with feigned reluctance. Surely you are familiar with the embarrassment of the tenor who, though he has been careful to bring his music roll to a party, must nevertheless affect a pretty surprise at being asked to sing . . . Now Gershwin would recognize no such silly necessity [i.e., to bring his own orchestra with him]. He is not merely a good pianist. He is a great one. No one knows this better than he does. Then he likes to play his own music. He cannot be bothered with the ritual of behavior which calls for his pretending otherwise.

However, such willingness to perform at the drop of a hat is characteristic of song writers. Indeed, George Kaufman, who had gone into a fruitful partnership with Gershwin in the evolving of such works as *Of Thee I Sing* and *Let 'em Eat Cake*, was once said to be arranging an interesting event for the next Olympic games. Twelve composers were to be lined up behind a tape. At a distance of a hundred yards, a tempting grand piano was to be wheeled into position, opened, set. Then, while myriad spectators sat tense, a pistol was to be fired and the race begun.

It was generally conceded that Gershwin would win, hands down. Hands down, that is, on the keyboard. Such artless readiness would irk Kaufman only when they were at work on a new show and George the Ingenuous would insist on playing the score in every drawing-

*Actually it was humorist and writer of light verse, Newman Levy.

room for weeks and months in advance. By the night of the anxious
New York première, everyone in the audience already would know it
by heart. Even the critics would hurry to their typewriters and, after
describing the insouciant gaiety of the new score, could not help
adding, 'To be sure, much of the music is reminiscent,' being vaguely
conscious, poor dears, that they had heard it before somewhere. Sometimes the sheer candor of Gershwin's self-examination more than ruf-
fled his colleagues. Sometimes it maddened them. There was the
instance of the rift with Harry Ruby, himself no mean songwriter but
even so, no Gershwin. They were playing ball together at Gershwin's
country place one summer when the game grew so rough that Gershwin
withdrew. His hands, he explained, were too valuable thus risked.

'Say,' said Ruby, 'What about *my* hands?'

'Well,' Gershwin replied, 'It's not the same thing.'

Over this disconcerting reply Ruby brooded in silence for a long
time, and in the process developed a reluctance to visit his erstwhile
crony. Indeed, they did not see each other again for two years. When
they did meet, it was by chance on the boardwalk at Atlantic City.

Gershwin was overjoyed at the reunion. Where had good old Ruby
been keeping himself? What was the matter anyway? Had he, Gershwin, said anything, done anything, to offend? After a moment's medi-
tation, and seeing that candor seemed *de rigueur*, Ruby decided to tell
him, and did so, relating the forgotten incident just as I have told it
to you. 'And then', he wound up, 'you said, "It's not the same thing." '

Gershwin received this in silence, took the story into the council-
chambers of his heart, examined it, and then replied, 'Well, it isn't.'*

---

*The story is true, but as was his wont, Woollcott embroiders the tale. In a letter (*c.*
1957–8) Ruby described the incident as lasting a few weeks. Ruby, a baseball addict, arrived
in Ossining, New York, where the Gershwins had rented an elaborate farmhouse in which
to work on the 1927 *Strike up the Band*. Guests visited frequently, among them Ruby, who
brought, as usual, his baseball accoutrements. Of all present, only Gershwin agreed to don
a glove and toss a few with the zealous Ruby. After a little practice, Gershwin decided to
quit, Ruby being good at throwing fast balls. That, in Woollcott's version, was when
Gershwin made the remark. According to Ruby he made it some weeks later in their
publisher's office. The competitive Gershwin agreed that Ruby had a great fastball, adding,
'I could do very well, also, if I tried, but I must be careful of my hands.' Then, as Ruby
wrote, 'in his sweet and natural way, with no insult intended, "with you it doesn't matter" '.
In chiding Gershwin about the comment at a party some time later, Ruby repeated the
remarks, Gershwin did not recall the incident; then, after some thought, said, 'Well, it's
true isn't it?' Ruby had no argument with that.

And of course he was so right. A similar habit of honest appraisal, I understand, complicated some of his romances. He is personable, free and thirty-six, and there were ever lovely ladies along his path. There was one girl he had rather meant to marry, but he never got around to telling her so. Meanwhile, she eloped with someone else. Gershwin was dining with friends when the news reached him. His head sank on his breast. In their respect for his manly grief, they let him be the first to speak. 'I'd feel terrible about this,' he said, 'if I weren't so busy right now.'

Then there was the girl who rather meant to marry him. The trouble was she had twice his musicianship. From the cradle she had learned to walk with Bach and the great ones. Inevitably she thought of him as less than Bach. He could scarcely quarrel with that, but he knew that such a point of view at close range was likely to keep him in an unproductive state of discouragement. Better to get a help-mate on a lower musical plane, one who did not know enough to realize his limitations. Gershwin's contribution to this familiar decision was to recognize the source of his discomfort, confess it cheerfully and rest upon it.

This ingenuousness also found its most frequent expression in relation to his painting. He has taken up the graphic art in a big way, spending long hours at his easel, looking up only to gaze meditatively over the rooftops of the magical city and wonder out loud whether he might not do well to give up music altogether in favor of oil and canvas. Since painting presented the more interesting problems, why not divert his indisputable talent from the one art to the other?

Meanwhile, there are many of his own works to be seen in his new home, affably sharing wall-space with little things by Utrillo, Renoir, and Cézanne, who are good painters, too. On the merits of these early Gershwins, I would not feel qualified to speak. My instinctive notion that they are godawful is tempered by a humbling knowledge that I feel the same way about many modern painting for possession of which our malfactors of great wealth pay through their respective noses.

[His] new home is a penthouse in East Seventy-Second Street, New York City, a bachelor apartment of fourteen rooms (counting the trunk-room). Its items include a great panelled reception hall, three pianos, and a bar that is a rhapsody in gaily colored glassware. A private telephone connects his workroom with the apartment across the street occupied by his brother, Ira Gershwin, who writes the words for his music. There is a sleeping porch equipped with strange jalousies. There are mysterious gadgets devised as substitutes for will power in setting-up exercises. There are flights of stairs that fold up and vanish at a touch . . .

As I finished my inspection of his luxurious new home one evening, I found myself struggling with a mischievous impulse to say, 'Ah, if instead of dying of starvation in a garret, Franz Schubert had had a place like this to work in, he might have amounted to something.'* I did suppress the impulse, but on my way home I fell to wondering what there was about Gershwin that incited me to such teasing – what, indeed there was to make faintly derisive, in intention at least, all the anecdotes people tell about him, of which I have here given only a sample handful. And it dawned on me that if we were all thus moved at times to a little urchin pebble-shying in his direction, it might be because of our knowledge – our uncomfortable, disquieting knowledge – that he is a genius.

Alexander Woollcott, 'George the Ingenuous', *Cosmopolitan*, November 1933, pp. 32–3, 122–3

---

*Another Woollcottism: Schubert neither starved to death nor died in a garret.

V
Getting to Know Him

Although he appears to have lived much of his life in public (for he was easily interviewed, accessible and seemed to be at frequent parties), Gershwin was a rather enigmatic personality. As his sister Frankie expressed it, his 'was a very closed-in personality, though he was very sweet and protective'. His devotion to work circumscribed a rounded personal life. It perplexed his friends that he never married; his detractors encumbered him with an enormous ego and his devotees found him 'kind' and 'exciting'. Many delighted in his boyish eagerness to play for hours on end at parties. Once when his mother warned him against overdoing this, he replied with 'the trouble is, when I don't play I don't have a good time'. As for that ego, Isaac Goldberg found him 'too essentially modest to make a pretence of modesty', although his 'frankness, at times, is a trifle breath-catching'. Goldberg told the story about Gershwin's invitation to visit the automobile capital, Detroit, in honour of a visit and celebration for 'one of the Infantas of Spain'. He was given a seat of honour 'near many automobile magnets, including Henry Ford'. When he returned, his friends and relatives 'expected a graphic account of the event – tales of Hispanic royalty and King Henry. 'I was a riot,' was his sole retort. 'I knocked them for a goal!' Obviously he had been asked to play.

Gershwin was not contentious and preferred writing new songs if a producer or vocalist decided against a song already in the show. He did not write letters complaining about unfair reviews. His friends, however, were more than willing to go to his defence. In 1932 an article appeared in the *American Spectator* entitled 'The Gershwin Myth', implying that Gershwin did not orchestrate his own concert works,* and that one of his ghost writers

*Gershwin orchestrated all his concert works after *Rhapsody in Blue*.

was his good friend, all-round musician and conductor, William Daly. The accuser, Allan Lincoln Langley, was a not very successful composer who made a living playing freelance in some of the major orchestras (notably the Boston Symphony and the New York Philharmonic). In his withering rebuttal, Daly said, 'I suppose I should really resent the fact that Langley attributes Gershwin's work to me, since Langley finds all of it so bad. But fortunately for my *amour propre*, I have heard some of Langley's compositions. He really should stay away from ink and stick to the viola.' Gershwin, he continued, 'receives many . . . suggestions from his many friends to whom he always plays his various compositions, light or symphonic, while they are in the process of being written. Possibly Mr Langley feels that we all get together (and we'd have to meet in the Yankee Stadium) and write Mr Gershwin's music for him.' Gershwin's large circle of friends was heterogeneous and came not only from the world of music and the theatre, but also from literature, finance, art and sport. Some have left their impressions of their co-worker and friend. Fascinating vignettes, journalistic, even trivial, illuminate various aspects of his personality. His brother Ira was closer to Gershwin than anyone; their relationship throughout was refreshingly free of sibling rivalry. Ira was willing to let George be *the* Gershwin and glowed in the reflection of his brother's celebrity. Later in his life, after retiring from songwriting, Ira Gershwin became an articulate guardian of his brother's works (preserving manuscripts, etc. in the Library of Congress) and his standing in American music.

CHARLES G. SHAW

(b. 1892)

An essayist whose writings, ranging from the personal ('Reveries of a Batchelor Nearing Forty') to the philosophical ('On Love and the Girls'), appeared in such prestigious publications as *The Bookman*, *The New Yorker* and *Vanity Fair*. He produced dozens of short 'profiles' of famed personalities of the 1920s from the world of sport, art and politics.

George Gershwin was born in Brooklyn, NY, and moved to Manhattan at the age of six weeks. He is the son of Morris and Rose Gershwin and a brother of Ira and Arthur. His sister is named Frances.

He never studied music until thirteen years old, and, as a boy was considered a hopeless case by his school teachers. He was, however, the champion roller skater of Seventh Street. He has no taste for poker but is fond of hearts, ping pong, golf, riding and, once in a while, a set of tennis. His tastes change every year.

Though his beard is a heavy one, he swears he would not shave twice a day for anything in the world. Now and then he will let it grow for three days – but no longer.

He ordinarily favors either a blue or grey suit, but never, under any conditions, a certain shade of brown. He will not wear American clothes . . .

From his workroom he gets an uninterrupted view of the Jersey soap factories.*

His favorite dish is bortsch, as brewed by his mother. He likewise evinces a lech for double lamb chops.

He believes that New York is the greatest city in the world for work, just as he prefers London for its calmness. Paris he loves for its beauty . . .

His particular dislikes are noisy people, 'sweet' music, garlic, crowds (save at his concerts) and alligator pears.

Marriage he considers to be the ideal state, and he remains a

---

*At this time Gershwin lived in a penthouse at 33 Riverside Drive, overlooking the Hudson River; he had a spectacular view of New Jersey's cliffs (known as the Palisades), and of downtown Manhattan.

bachelor merely because the right girl has not yet come along. He thinks marriage has so often failed due to a lack of vision, and he compares unhappily married couples to fine musicians who write flabby music.

He regards movies, on the whole, as a waste of time.

He is attracted to horses and dogs, and relishes the dramatic confections of Bernard Shaw. His favorite modern literary piece is 'Porgy'.

Unless a day be set, on which his work must be finished, he will linger over it for months. He is not in the least methodical and works according to mood.*

He likes ice cream sodas and Scotch highballs, with a casual cocktail on the side, but rarely touches loganberry juice. Don Sebastians are his favorite cigars.

His complexion is ruddy and his hair a deep sable.

He will often work for twelve hours without stopping, during which time he becomes so engrossed that he suffers from a nervous indigestion. Beyond these spells his health doesn't trouble him.

For relaxation he visits an osteopath.

When in the mood, he can work anywhere, regardless of the size, shape, or color of the room. His 'Rhapsody in Blue' – finished in three weeks – was written in an Amsterdam Avenue apartment to the jangle of bus and trolley lines. On the other hand, he hates the croaking of bull-frogs in the country.

He loves a good prize-fight.

Supper clubs bore him numb, and though fond of dancing, he finds himself taking in fewer and fewer parties every year. Among his most prized possessions are an autographed photo of Prince George of England (signed 'From George to George') and a gold cigarette case (bearing the signatures of twenty-eight of his friends) presented to him by Otto Kahn, at a party, after a performance of his Concerto.†

He seldom smokes cigarettes, save in feminine company, but will not infrequently tackle a pipe.

He finds it very hard to be on time.

To discover the perfect medium with which to express his ideas in

---

*Not quite the Gershwin that others knew.

†Kahn was a financier-patron; he was associated with the New York Philharmonic (as president) and the Metropolitan Opera (1907–34). His effort to present Gershwin's *Porgy and Bess* at the Metropolitan was not successful!

music he believes to be his aim in life. He would sacrifice much, he says, to achieve sufficient technique by which to record these ideas.

As for 'blues', he prefers the lowest musical form. He has broken the house record in attendance at the Lewisohn Stadium, when eighteen thousand admirers on July 25, 1927, assembled to hear one of his concerts.

Politics interest him not in the least. Neither is he drawn to masculine women.

It is impossible to predict, he thinks, what shape music will take a hundred years from now, though whatever happens, he believes, there will be no improvement upon Bach.

He is also of the opinion that the world's auricular senses are growing more refined and that a keener appreciation of sounds exists to-day than ever before.

He considers his greatest thrill hearing one of his orchestral pieces played precisely as he felt while writing it.

He devours a plate of cornflakes and bran every night before going to bed.

His greatest devotions are his dog, Tinker, and his family. He sits in on all his show rehearsals, helping with the casting, direction, and stage business in general. He is a shrewd judge of people, usually adhering to his initial impressions.

He likes his producers and believes them to be always right.

His cheques and bills are all made out by his brother, Ira. Otherwise they would be forgotten and remain unpaid. Ira also answers most of his mail and telegrams. It is only recently that he was persuaded to hire a secretary. Easily shocked, his conversation – especially with women – almost borders on the Puritanical.

His usual working uniform consists of a pair of pajamas, a bathrobe and slippers.

He admires Igor Stravinsky, Bill Daly, Edgar Selwyn,* and Max Beerbohm, just as he heartily envies the first-edition libraries of MM. [B. G.] de Sylva and Jerome Kern, though he makes no attempt to duplicate them.

He always plays when asked to, and will sit at the piano for hours to an audience of one or a thousand.

*Broadway producer of both productions of *Strike up the Band* (1927, a failure; and 1930, a success). Selwyn eventually settled in Hollywood as a producer of films.

He is more amused by his father's unconscious humor than by that of the world's most side-splitting comedians, and has made the gags of Gershwin *père* classics along Broadway.*

Of his entire family he was the first to show the slightest musical talent.

Charles G. Shaw, *The Low-Down* (New York, 1928), pp. 151–9

MERLE ARMITAGE

(1893–1975)

Impresario and civil engineer turned designer and author, Armitage was closely associated with Gershwin in the composer's last years; he presented the first all-Gershwin concert in Los Angeles in February 1937. It was during a rehearsal and during a performance that Gershwin first experienced the symptoms of the brain tumor that would take his life. At the time of his death he and Armitage were discussing a revival of *Porgy and Bess*.

George Gershwin was proud that he was an American. When he said, 'My people are American; my time is today – music must repeat the thought and aspirations of the times' – he was giving verbal utterance to a quality his music invariably expresses . . . The excitement, the nervousness and the movement of America were natural motivations in Gershwin's life and in Gershwin's music. It is a commonplace that during his lifetime his music had little discerning critical appraisal. Admirers and friends, the thousands who had fallen in love with his music, distorted judgements – crowded out the possibility and opportunity for detached, considered evaluations. And while Gershwin may not be destined for the exalted sphere which some of his fatuous followers prophesied, his importance is immeasurably greater than has been imagined by many in High Places. And the only logical explanation of this remarkable range of evaluation is that George confused both camps because he was unique . . .

---

*One of his favourites: overhearing George and Ira discussing Einstein and his theory and George commenting, 'Imagine, working for twenty years on an idea and then being able to write it down in three pages.' – 'It was probably very small print,' was Morris Gershwin's contribution.

America had almost overcome its musical inferiority complex, through its possession of more first class symphony orchestras than could be heard in all of Europe, when its smugness suffered a slight shock. A denizen of Tin Pan Alley was first tolerated, then *invited* into the temples of great music! . . .

Although many European critics had long since recognized the vitality of American jazz, and had written of the extreme probability that jazz and the technique of jazz would affect the future, we were too complacent with our foreign importations to risk admiring a home-grown product, and much too unsure of its importance – at least many of us were . . .

Into this milieu the figure of George Gershwin was projected. Already, in certain quarters, he was damned, for he had written the outrageously successful *Swanee* for Al Jolson and several of *George White's Scandals*. One of the *Scandals* so impressed Paul Whiteman, who longed to take jazz into the concert halls, that he invited George to contribute to that certain Aeolian Hall concert on February 12, 1924, when the world first heard the *Rhapsody in Blue* . . .

The advent of Gershwin gave rise to a curious attitude on the part of certain people in the musical world. One school of thought held that jazz after all might contain something of value, but that only a Wagner or a Debussy of today, or as they implied, a *real* composer, could make important use of it. Another school, of course, banned it altogether. But certain influential people of discernment believed that Gershwin *was a real* composer – and knew that his music was well founded. There is an attitude which has gained some credence, that the 'larger' Gershwin works will not live, that only his songs and less pretentious compositions have the seed of immortality . . .

If one wished to sum up George Gershwin as an artist, his own label could well be used. He spoke of himself as a 'modern romantic'. His music expresses it; his own painting exudes it . . . As a man, George Gershwin had qualities of heart and mind which were extremely ingratiating. He was entirely sincere. His ability to achieve a good bargain in a business sense resulted from his protecting his own very generous nature. He always seemed to be in balance. He had a very definite idea of his place in the world and of his importance as an artist – yet he was modest. I have seen him blush at flattery. Although he presented a somewhat cold exterior, I have known the inner warmth of his friendship. George Gershwin possessed a love of Broadway, the admiration of the motion picture industry, and the respect of the serious musical world – an unparalleled accomplishment. He had one supreme quality, without which everything else would have availed little. He had style!

Merle Armitage, 'George Gershwin and His Time', *George Gershwin*, Merle Armitage, ed. (New York, 1938), pp. 5–8, 11, 13–15

George was always the recipient of a good deal of good-natured and sometimes astringent comment because of his preoccupation with music. George S. Kaufman's gentle remark, 'I'd bet on George anytime – in a hundred-yard dash to the piano', and Oscar Levant's acid question, 'Tell me, George, if you had it to do all over again – would you still fall in love with yourself?' are typical. But neither of these close friends really meant this witty spoofing. Bennett Cerf came closer to the truth when he observed: 'I have never seen a man happier, more bursting with the sheer joy of living, than George was when he was playing his songs.' . . .

Proof of George's modesty was his interest and devotion to *all* music. He was an exceptionally informed man. His love for and knowledge of the chamber music of Mozart, Brahms and Debussy, his deep feeling for the Mozart operas, are examples. He was familiar with almost everything written by Bach and Beethoven. He explored the world of Rameau, Pergolesi, Palestrina and Gluck. But the greatest masters were like *old masters* hanging in a museum. Full of admiration for them, he was nevertheless going in another direction, his direction. And while grateful for the rich heritage from Palestrina to Bartók, and very excited about the men of his time, Schoenberg, Ravel, Milhaud, Hindemith, Berg, Stravinsky, he knew he belonged in still another world. But his interest in Berg, for instance, was so serious that he took time from his heavy schedule to go to the *Wozzeck* performance in Philadelphia.

Merle Armitage, *George Gershwin – Man and Legend* (New York, 1958), p. 73

SIR OSBERT SITWELL

(1892–1969)

An old Etonian and member of an exceptional literary family, Osbert Sitwell was best known as a short-story writer and novelist (author of the outstanding *Before the Bombardment*, 1926), who also produced several witty and wise autobiographical works. Sitwell collaborated with Sir William Walton on the latter's oratorio, *Belshazzar's Feast*.

Though Gershwin was not an intimate friend of mine, I knew him and liked him, and he would usually come to have luncheon with us when he visited London. He possessed a fine racial appearance; nobody could mistake him for anyone but a Jew. Tall and vigorous, his clearly cut face with its handsome ram's head, the features prominent, but, as it were, streamlined, indicated will power, character, and talent. I have always understood that he was the son of immigrants from Russia or Germany and was brought up in the poorest quarter of New York:* but his manners were notably excellent, his voice was pleasant, and though the force of his personality was plain in his whole air, he was modest in bearing, and I never noticed a trace of the arrogance with which he has been credited. Many of his contemporaries, it may be, attributed an exaggerated value to his celebrated *Rhapsody in Blue*, but at least the hundreds of songs and dances he wrote are altogether typical in their audacity of the age that gave them birth, so expert of their kind, and no chronicle on the epoch could fail to mention them and their pervasive influence.

Sir Osbert Sitwell, *Laughter in the Next Room* (London, 1949)

PAUL WHITEMAN

There is an especial place in my heart for George Gershwin, and that place is his alone. Before Gershwin there were hundreds of great songwriters. They were not inartistic in their compositions, but they

---

*When the Gershwins lived in New York's Lower East Side, it was not the slum that it later became; their way of life was closer to middle-class and, unlike another Lower East Sider, Irving Berlin, they never experienced real poverty.

had not touched the field that awaited his particular genius. What I am attempting to say is that there is nothing in their contributions from the technical side of music or musical development that would give reason for the so-called jazz type to be included in the concert field. It remained for Gershwin to give dignity to a medium of expression that had before him been held in slight contempt. His rare originality, coupled with his keen grasp of the orchestra, always was shown in his piano playing. He thought always in orchestral terms, and he played in that fashion . . .

I feel that George Gershwin was more than ever just commencing to come into his own. With his knowledge and skill he wrote numbers that have become musical milestones. He was a great example of the merging of hit qualities with intelligent musicianship. He led the way. He has given the finer jazz a firm root – so firm a root that others who come after him may carry on his fine reputation. The Gershwin *theme* has been inculcated in the minds of the younger composers, and it is for them to take it, and go forward . . .

George Gershwin was the highest type of character. He is gone – but his music is his enduring monument.

Paul Whiteman, 'George and the Rhapsody', *George Gershwin*, Merle Armitage, ed. (New York, 1938), pp. 24–6

WALTER DAMROSCH
(1862–1950)

German-born, he came from a musical family (both his father, Leopold, and his brother, Frank, were conductors). The family came to the US in 1871 and all became members of the musical community. By the age of twenty, Walter was conductor of the Newark (New Jersey) Harmonic Society; in 1885 he succeeded his father as conductor of the Oratorio Society and the Symphony Society of New York, a precursor, with the Philharmonic Society, of today's New York Philharmonic. As conductor of the Society, Damrosch introduced his audiences to the new works of Brahms, Tchaikovsky and Wagner. A musical conservative, he commissioned works by contemporary

American composers. As a composer he is best known for his setting of Kipling's 'Danny Deever' and several operas, among them, *The Scarlet Letter* (1896) and *The Man Without a Country* (1937). Damrosch was a pioneer in the broadcasting of concert music via radio in the 1930s.

It was in 1925 that I first became attracted by George Gershwin and the music which he had composed for various Broadway productions. It showed such originality both of melodic invention and harmonic progressions that I strongly felt that he had in him the possibility of development on more serious lines. I suggested to the president of the New York Symphony Society, Mr Harry Harkness Flagler, that it might be a lovely and important inducement for his artistic future to commission him to write a piano concerto for the Symphony Society, which should have its first performance at one of our concerts, he to play the piano part. Mr Flagler heartily agreed with this suggestion and George Gershwin wrote the concerto for us and received almost unanimous and enthusiastic acclaim for the work on its production on December 3, 1925. I still think that the second movement of this concerto, with its dreamy atmosphere of a summer night in a garden of our South, reaches a high water mark of his talent.

I developed a strong affection for him personally, and for the genuineness of his musical talent. He had an almost child-like affection and pride for his own music. To tell the truth, I tried to wean him, so to speak, from Broadway, as I felt that he had it in him to develop on more serious lines than the Broadway musical shows demanded or even permitted. But the lure of lighter forms in which he had become such a master, proved too strong. Perhaps I was wrong and his own instinct guided him towards what he felt most able to do. In the end it must be an inner urge which compels our artistic destinies.

Walter Damrosch, 'Gershwin and the Concerto in F', *George Gershwin*, Merle Armitage, ed. (New York, 1938), pp. 32–3.

Since then [1925] he wrote innumerable and exquisite songs, and a delightful orchestral poem, 'An American in Paris', gay, picturesque and full of humor, of which I gave the first performance in New York. Personally, George Gershwin was a man of infinite charm and with an almost touching delight in his own music. He was happiest when sitting at the piano, surrounded by my children and their friends, singing and playing dozens of his own songs. His all too early death was a real tragedy for American music. He was still young, and throughout his typically American career, he gave continual proof of his rare genius.

Walter Damrosch, 'Gershwin and his Music', *Rhapsody in Blue, The Jubilant Story of George Gershwin and his Music*, Warner Brothers promotional brochure (Hollywood, 1945)

MARIO BRAGGIOTTI
(b. 1909)

Born in Italy, educated at the New England Conservatory, Mario Braggiotti was studying with Nadia Boulanger at Fontainebleau when he first met Gershwin. He later became a member of the duo piano team of (Jacques) Fray and Braggiotti. The team appeared in the pit of the London production of *Funny Face*. Braggiotti eventually settled in New York and was active as duo pianist (with Fray) and as soloist, in radio and as a composer.

When I was studying at the Paris Conservatory of Music during the roaring twenties, I read one morning of the arrival of the young American composer, George Gershwin, who had come to Paris seeking inspiration for his new ballet commissioned by Florenz Zeigfeld.* As the Gershwin fan that I was (and never will cease to be) I unhesitatingly went up to his [Majestic] hotel suite and boldly introduced myself as a fellow musician. Attired in a working dressing gown, Gershwin gaily ushered me inside with that vague and stunned manner of one who was holding tightly to the thread of a creative mood. Beside his Steinway was a group of bridge tables covered with all sizes and makes of French taxi horns. George, suddenly oblivious of my presence, sat down in front of his manuscript and quickly finished a musical sentence that my bell ringing had interrupted; then he turned to me as I stared

---

*Gershwin had no commission for this work; he merely wanted to write. Upon its completion both Leopold Stokowski and Walter Damrosch wanted to première it. When Stokowski heard about Damrosch, he lost interest. *An American in Paris* was used as a ballet in the Ziegfeld production, *Show Girl* (1929).

at the funny horns: 'I'm looking for the right horn pitch for the street scene of a ballet I'm writing. Calling it *An American in Paris*. Lots of fun. I think I've got something. Just finished sketching the slow movement.' He paused and looked at the piano music rack with the elated expression of a mother regarding her new cradle. 'Here, I want to try this accompaniment. Won't you play the melody in the treble?' Flattered and eager, I moved swiftly beside him at the piano. He started the two-bar vamp and I joined in, reading the single-note lead from his fresh manuscript. And, for the first time anywhere, there echoed the amazingly original and nostalgic slow movement of 'An American in Paris', undoubtedly one of Gershwin's most brilliant works. George chewingly switched his perennial cigar from mouth left to mouth right and said, 'How do you like it?' . . . He was the most modest of men, and he let his music and his performance of it speak for him. The best possible pointers one could get from Gershwin came from sitting nearby and listening to him play. And this I was lucky enough to do very often – through a long period during which he used to hold weekly open house evenings in his studio. These were stimulating parties where a nucleus of composers, pianists, conductors, singers, etc. would gather around the Gershwin pianos and anything might happen, from a new blues to the discussion of a recent prize-fight, a sport of which George was an ardent fan. And inevitably of course he would play.

Gershwin had the light, incisive touch, the poetic melodies and sure sense of rhythm that gave what he wrote its shape, its weight and its color. All the pedagogic pointers in the world were there for anyone who cared to listen. His pedalling was extraordinarily subtle, and he never sacrificed anything at the expense of rhythm. He always had a climax to his phrasing as if he were telling a thought with a convincing punch line. And his singing tone has a nostalgic quality and an unpredictable texture that I have never heard equaled. His playing carried intuitively the great overall secret of all forms of projection – whether they be in music, elocution or athletics – in one word, control. Actually the only thing during his performances which he couldn't control was the enthusiasm of his listeners.

Mario Braggiotti, 'Gershwin is here to stay', *Etude*, February 1953, p. 14

ISAAC GOLDBERG

I rarely attended the parties that Gershwin gave in his various New York homes. It was a joke between us that I had a standing invitation not to come to any party that he gave. I preferred the more intimate moments, when I might listen to his aims, his wonders, his doubts. From the first I had felt that he was not the man to pursue an intensive course in academic music . . . Gershwin was [like his] music, honest, real, forthright, unaffected, basically sound . . . George had an intense desire to write a few bars of music that would live. The question, 'Do you think anything of mine will live?' was often on his lips.

Isaac Goldberg, 'Homage to a Friend', *George Gershwin*, Merle Armitage, ed. (New York, 1938), pp. 163–4

ABRAM CHASINS
(1903–87)

> Abram Chasins studied with Ernest Hutcheson and Rubin Goldmark at the Juilliard School of Music. After a successful career as a piano soloist, often performing his own works, including two piano concertos, he joined the staff of 'good music' radio station WQXR, New York, as music consultant, and was appointed director in 1965. His books include *Speaking of Pianists*, *The Van Cliburn Legend* and *Stokie* [Stokowski], *the Incredible Apollo*. He was a lifelong friend of the Gershwin family.

The durability of the *Rhapsody in Blue*, Concerto in F, and *An American in Paris* must be puzzling to those who never quite certified George Gershwin. Internationally, and for over a quarter of a century now, these works, despite their obvious organizational defects, have exerted a magnetic power to pull throngs into concert halls. But it takes a naïveté equal to Gershwin's esthetics to attribute his prestige merely to the banal taste or imperfect culture of a vast audience. It fails to explain why – suddenly in Gershwin – form and matter, means and ends, are not quite the inseparables we thought they were. It seems evident that in Gershwin's large-form works, the telling accident of genius has clearly outweighed every theoretical and technical issue. Otherwise there seems to me no sound explanation for the phenomenal and abiding impact of his music.

In the small song-form Gershwin is the complete master. In his inimitable musical-comedy and film scores, his music holds long scenes together admirably. Here we remember that he worked with the aid of expert collaborators – notably brother Ira, an artist in his own right. *Porgy and Bess* is a throbbing masterpiece, for all its unorthodoxies. It is in the instrumental works that Gershwin's ideas are framed within formulas, hampered from taking full flight with that freedom which stems only from solid knowledge and inexorable discipline.

Gershwin's achievements are far beyond those attainable by technical processes alone. He had inspiration, the lifegiving element in art. A work without it, no matter how perfectly constructed, cannot endure. Inspiration may inhabit a march or a mass. It may pervade a potboiler or a masterpiece. It still remains the magic to which the great heart of the public is as susceptible as the most exacting expert.

Abram Chasins, 'Paradox in Blue', *Saturday Review of Literature*, 25 February 1956, pp. 37–8, 64–6

VERNON DUKE

(1903–69)

Born Vladimir Dukelsky, he fled the Russian Revolution of 1920 and arrived in New York a year later, where he met Gershwin who suggested his new, anglicized name. Duke wrote popular songs under his new name, and concert music (no less than three symphonies, violin and cello concertos and chamber works – now rarely heard) as Dukelsky. He is most renowned for such songs as 'April in Paris' (lyric by E. Y. Harburg), 'I can't get started' (Ira Gershwin) and 'Taking a chance on love' (John Latouche and Ted Fetter).

When I informed him of my years with Reinhold Glière, the difficulty I had had mastering counterpoint and orchestration at fifteen, he was vaguely impressed. 'Gee, it must be great to know so much,' he said, eyeing me with curiosity. 'But now that you've learned it all – what are you doing with it?' By way of reply I played an extremely cerebral piano sonata. Gershwin listened, rather impatiently, I thought, and then shook his head. 'There's no money in that kind of stuff,' he said, 'no heart in it, either. Try to write some real popular tunes – and don't be scared about going low-brow. They will open you up!'

Vernon Duke, *Passport to Paris* (Boston, 1955), p. 90

S. N. BEHRMAN
(1893–1973)

S. N. Behrman was the author of some twenty plays, among them *The Second Man* (1927), *End of the Summer* (1936) and *No Time for Comedy*. In collaboration with Joshua Logan he wrote the book for the musical *Fanny* (songs by Harold Rome). His non-fiction works include the biographies *Duveen* (1952) and *Max* (Beerbohm, 1960) and several autobiographical volumes. His best-known screenplays were written for Greta Garbo: *Queen Christina* (1933) and *Anna Karenina* (1935).

George's life was lived so out-of-doors, so in the public eye, and these activities so absorbed him that he was always 'too busy', he said, for introspective agonies. He told me once that he wanted to write for young girls sitting on fire escapes on hot summer nights in New York and dreaming of love.

S. N. Behrman, *People in a Diary* (Boston, 1972), p. 256

VERNON DUKE

On May 29th [1928], I took [Sergei] Diaghilev and Prokofiev to hear Gershwin's Piano Concerto played by Dimitri Tiomkin at a concert in the Paris Opera conducted by Vladimir Golschmann. Whether the fault lay with the French musicians, notoriously allergic to jazz, or with Mr Tiomkin, an able pianist but certainly no Gershwin, I cannot say. Diaghilev shook his head and muttered something about 'good jazz and bad Liszt,' whereas Prokofiev, intrigued by some of the pianistic invention, asked me to bring George to his apartment the next day. George came and played his head off; Prokofiev liked the tunes and the flavorsome embellishments, but thought little of the concerto (repeated by Gershwin), which, he said later, consisted of 32–bar choruses ineptly bridged together. He thought highly of his gifts, both as composer and pianist, however, and predicted that he'd go far should he leave 'dollars and dinners' alone.

Vernon Duke, *Passport to Paris* (Boston, 1955), p. 209

S. N. BEHRMAN

George was becoming one of the most eligible bachelors in America; there was curiosity among his friends from the beginning as to who the girl would be. I began hearing about the 'Dream Girl'. The Dream Girl was a Chicago physical culture teacher whom I never met. She gave George physical workouts, which he thought were good for him. Physical well-being led to infatuation . . . We waited for a wedding announcement. It didn't come; it kept on being delayed. Years passed. One day Ira called me to tell me some devastating news: 'Dream Girl' (we never referred to her in any other way: I never knew her name) was married! He hadn't the heart to tell George. He begged me to relieve him of this disagreeable chore. I took on the job . . . 'George,' I said, 'I have bad news for you. Dream Girl is married.' His brown eyes showed a flicker of pain. He kept looking at me. Finally he spoke.

'Do you know?' he said, 'if I weren't so busy I'd feel terrible.'

S. N. Behrman, *People in a Diary*, (Boston, 1972), p. 246

OSCAR LEVANT

(1906–72)

Pianist, composer, film actor and author, Levant was also known for his wide-ranging erudition and acrid wit. He came from Pittsburgh in the mid-twenties, met Gershwin and became one of his finest interpreters. Influenced by Gershwin he tried his hand at writing songs, with no great success, except for 'Lady, play your mandolin' (lyric by

Irving Caesar). His concert works, written under the
influence of his teacher, Arnold Schoenberg, include a
piano concerto, two sonatinas for piano, two string quartets, orchestral suites, and a *Dirge*, dedicated to Gershwin.
Levant's film career began in the mid-forties when he
appeared as himself in the quasi-film biography of Gershwin, *Rhapsody in Blue*. Other films include *The Barkleys
of Broadway*, *An American in Paris* and *The Bandwagon*.

A friend relates that the evening of the concert* chanced to coincide
with the hottest day of an unbearably hot New York summer . . .
Despite the oppressive heat that lingered after sundown a large crowd
appeared for the concert at which George both conducted and played.

During the intermission the friend wandered backstage to exchange
a greeting with George, to find him in conversation with Mrs Charles
Guggenheimer, director of the Stadium concerts. She [was] exuding
enthusiasm . . . but George seemed detached and inattentive. When
she paused for a moment he said, 'How's the crowd?'

'Grand,' she answered, 'More than twelve thousand.'

With a shake of his head, Gershwin observed, 'Last year we had
seventeen thousand.'

The friend interrupted, 'Don't forget, George – this was the hottest
day in the history of New York.' He brightened at this and remarked,
with that curious mixture of irrelevance and seriousness, 'That's right,
I know four friends who were supposed to come, but they were
overcome by the heat.'

Oscar Levant, *A Smattering of Ignorance* (New York, 1941), pp. 167–8

VERNON DUKE

The Gershwins then [*c*. 1930] lived at 33 Riverside Drive in adjoining
penthouses. George's was breathtakingly modern, with all the latest
mechanical refinements and a fully equipped gymnasium. His *cabinet
de travail* boasted a huge Steinway and a spectacular view of the
Hudson, also a collection of modern paintings, to which some of his
own (he painted remarkably well) were periodically added. Parties,
again, were the order of the night and I, already a veteran party

*9 and 10 July 1936; Gershwin's last Lewisohn Stadium appearance.

boy, attended regularly . . . Among the regulars were Bill Daly, Gershwin's favorite pit conductor, elfin Kay Swift, whose 'Can't we be friends' and 'Fine and dandy', promised a bright Broadway career, and the professional sourpuss, Oscar Levant, a good-hearted neurotic.

Vernon Duke, *Passport to Paris* (Boston, 1955), pp. 222–3

OSCAR LEVANT

The pleasure I had in appearing on the program with George* was only exceeded by the little unpremeditated expressions of his reactions to the concert. It was hardly over when one of his truly well-disposed friends rushed back, wrung his hand and said, 'George, it was wonderful!'

'That's all?' said George, with characteristic abstraction. 'Just wonderful?'

Oscar Levant, *A Smattering of Ignorance* (New York, 1941), p. 165

VERNON DUKE

When not playing ping-pong on the ground floor [of his five storey house on West 103rd Street] with brothers Ira or Arthur, George could be found at the piano, playing tirelessly for hours, never practising in the Czerny sense, just racing through new tunes, adding new tricks, harmonies, 'first and second endings' and changing keys after every chorus. He was a born *improvisatore*.

Vernon Duke, *Passport to Paris* (Boston, 1955), p. 93

ROUBEN MAMOULIAN
(1898–1987)

Russian-born, Mamoulian was active in the theatre and films; he directed both versions of *Porgy and Bess*. He also was director of *Oklahoma!* (1943), *Carousel* (1945), *St Louis Woman* (1946) and *Lost in the Stars* (1949). His films include *Love Me Tonight* (1932), *Becky Sharp* (1935) and *Silk Stockings* (1957).

*The all-Gershwin concert, Lewisohn Stadium, New York, 16 August, 1932.

The first time I met George Gershwin was in late 1923 in Rochester, NY, where I had recently arrived from Europe to direct operas at the Eastman Theatre . . .

My first impression of Gershwin during that evening was that of a rather worried and anxious young man – very ambitious and not very happy. Rather reserved and self-centered and in some curious way suspicious of the world, looking not unlike a child with more apples than he can comfortably hold in his hands and afraid that someone would take them away from him . . .

George's attitude towards himself and his work was apt to be misunderstood by people who did not know him well. Because he liked his own music and praised himself, some of them thought he was conceited. This was not so, as I myself discovered. Conceit is made of much sterner stuff – it was not that with George. It was his faculty to look at himself and his work in just as detached a manner as if he were looking at somebody else. George had a tremendous capacity for appreciation and enthusiasm and always gave it generous expression in words. Whatever he liked, he praised it without any self-consciousness or false modesty . . .

George was so completely naïve and innocent in his liking his own work that it actually became one of the endearing qualities of his nature. Some little expressions that would seem arrogant coming from other men were touching and lovable when coming from George . . .

George loved playing the piano for people and would do at the slightest provocation. At any gathering of friends, if there was a piano in the room, George would play it. I am sure that most of his friends in thinking of George at his best, think of George at the piano. I've heard many pianists and composers play for informal gatherings, but I know of no one who did it with such genuine delight and verve. Just as the few chosen people are blessed with *joie de vivre* so was George blessed with the joy of playing the piano. George at the piano was George happy. He would draw a lovely melody out of the keyboard like a golden thread, then he would play with it and juggle it, twist it and toss it around mischievously, weave it into unexpected intricate patterns, tie it in knots and untie it and hurl it into a cascade of ever changing rhythms and counterpoints . . .

George was like a child. He had a child's innocence and imagination. He could look at the same thing ever so many times and yet see it anew every time he looked at it and enjoy it . . . Yet at times he was like a patriarch. I would look at him and all but see a long white beard and a staff in his hand. This would usually happen whenever a group of people around him argued violently about something. George would smile and look at them as though they were little children. His face would seem to say, 'You are all such lovely people and you are all a little foolish in your loud excitement. You are sweet to be so vehement and I really love you for it – but stop now – you've had enough.' He was old then and wise and tolerant. A patriarch. The simple gaiety of a child and the clear serenity of the old were two extremities of George's character. In between there was much of him that was neither simple nor clear, nor perhaps as happy. George did not live easily. He was a complicated, nervous product of our age. There was in him an intricate and restless combination of intellectual and emotional forces. Conflicting impulses clashed within him and played havoc. Nor was he free of complexes and inhibitions. These he always tried to analyze . . .

With all this George had a keen and joyous sense of humor. His was not the limited sense of humor which merely loves a funny story and is able to recognize one. It was the deeper sense of noticing the amusing in everything that happens in life, around oneself and within oneself. The stories he told with affectionate amusement about people in the street, his friends, his own family, would fill a book. He kept his sense of humor even in relation to things that were of utmost importance to him. Once, during a very earnest discussion of psycho-analysis, I asked him, 'Tell me, George, how much does a psycho-analyst usually charge?' George smiled and answered, 'He finds out how much you make and then charges you more than you can afford!'*

Rouben Mamoulian, 'I Remember', *George Gershwin*, Merle Armitage, ed. (New York, 1938), pp. 47–57

*Gershwin underwent analysis with Dr Gregory Zilboorg for about a year during 1934–5. He was introduced by his good friend composer Kay Swift, who, with her husband James Warburg, was also seeing Zilboorg. Swift now feels that it was one of the most unfortunate suggestions she ever made to Gershwin. Zilboorg seems to have resented the composer, who was merely curious about psychoanalysis and himself, not a neurotic with a mother complex, as has been suggested.

ISAAC GOLDBERG

Something in him, even on the threshold of forty, remained eternally boyish. There was a look in his eyes that was the counterpart of his frequent doubts . . . I recall once . . . that I was taking moving pictures of him in the Public Gardens (Boston). He noticed a heap of dirt by a flower bed. Seizing a twig, he stood before the dirt heap and posed in caricature fashion, as I cranked the camera. 'And what's that idea?' I asked. 'Call it Gershwin conducting some of his rubbish,' he said. This was simply an extreme statement of the way he sometimes felt about his musical gropings. George, of course, never regarded his least work as 'rubbish'.

Isaac Goldberg, 'Homage to a Friend', *George Gershwin*, Merle Armitage, ed. (New York, 1938), p. 165

OSCAR LEVANT

To my astonishment I found Gershwin amazingly accessible at his apartment on 110th Street. When I arrived he was working on the first movement of 'our' concerto with the late Bill Daly, his devoted friend and favorite conductor. I had scarcely accustomed myself to the reality of his presence when I realized that he was halfway through playing the new work.

I was bristling and stammered some graceless remark. George mistook my confusion and admiration for disapproval, which in turn made him involuntarily hostile. In addition to the work itself, his swift and mettlesome piano playing had so stimulated and excited me that the old dormant envy was reborn. He was merely annoyed and returned to his work. I left, having successfully made my usual bad impression . . .

[Leonore Gershwin] suggested that perhaps I would like to spend the evening with George and [her husband] Ira, and I escorted her to the apartment house on Riverside Drive, where the Gershwins occupied adjoining penthouses. These were connected by a short passageway that facilitated their work together and also the mutual interchange of guests. The house was mostly filled with an element of parasites, both esthetic and gustatory. Here I discovered I was a born leader, for I soon took charge of this hitherto disorganized group . . .

From the first day's supper I worked up to having four or five meals a day with the Gershwins, eating my way through the composition of the music and lyrics for *Delicious* and *Girl Crazy*. Out of sheer perverseness, I felt, George would cajole me frequently to leave the wonderful savory dishes on Ira's table to share with him a menu suited to his favorite ailment – 'composer's stomach'. It consisted of gruel (and such variants as oatmeal and farina), rusk, zwieback, melba toast (only on festive occasions), Ry-krisp, Swedish bread and Rusk. The *pièce de résistance* was stewed fruit or, when he was in a gluttonous mood, apple sauce . . .

Once I had been admitted to George's friendship I took so much pleasure in the things he was writing and doing that I did nothing of my own . . . Listening to him improvise and play was enough for me. He had such fluency at the piano and so steady a surge of ideas that any time he sat down just to amuse himself something came of it. Actually this is how he got most of his ideas – just by playing. He enjoyed writing so much because, in a sense, it was play for him – the thing he liked to do more than anything else . . .

We took a late train for the overnight trip, sharing a drawing room. A lengthy discussion on music occupied us for an hour or so, and I was actually in the midst of answering one of his questions when he calmly removed his clothes and eased himself into the lower berth . . . There was nothing left for me to do but undress and attempt to finish my sentence as I did. George, however, resumed the thread of his discourse, and I suggested perhaps it was difficult for him to sleep on a train and would he like one of my sleeping pills with the air of a man offering a friend an after-dinner mint.

I adjusted myself to the inconveniences of the upper berth, reflecting on the artistic–economic progressing by which Paderewski has a private car, Gershwin a drawing room and Levant a sleepless night. At this moment my light must have disturbed George's doze, for he opened his eyes, looked up at me and said drowsily, 'Upper berth – lower berth. That's the difference between talent and genius.'

Oscar Levant, *A Smattering of Ignorance* (New York, 1941), pp. 160, 169–70

VERNON DUKE

Prokofiev and I went to the *Strike up the Band* opening and later to a midnight party at the Warburgs,* where there was no room for nostalgia but where the music was better: George didn't leave the piano until the notices – all excellent – arrived, then resumed his recital with renewed vigor. At the party Pop Gershwin distinguished himself twice: when Russel Crouse asked him how he like the show, he parried with: 'What you mean how I like it? I *have* to like it.' And again, when George introduced him to Roger Pryor,† the leading man, Pop remarked benignly: 'Oh yes, you were on the American side.' (*Strike up the Band* had to do with an imaginary war between the US and Switzerland.)

Vernon Duke, *Passport to Paris* (Boston, 1955), p. 234

S. N. BEHRMAN

He also had a knack for making enigmatic remarks. One of them I puzzled over for years without hitting on an explanation. I was walking up Broadway on a hot August night with George. The papers were full of the sensation of the moment: the announced engagement of Irving Berlin to Ellin Mackay.‡ George and I were deep in it. He stopped suddenly, gave me an earnest look, and said: 'You know, I think it's a bad thing for all songwriters.'

S. N. Behrman, *People in a Diary* (Boston, 1972), p. 245

FRANCES GERSHWIN GODOWSKY

George was a fine dancer; he was so well coordinated and very graceful. He moved very well. He often took me dancing and we had a lot of

*James Paul Warburg, the financier, was married to Kay Swift at this time; using the pseudonym Paul James, he wrote lyrics to her melodies. Her relationship with Gershwin, which began in 1926, ended the Warburg marriage.
†Actually Jerry Goff, leading juvenile in the 1930 version; Pryor had the role in the 1927 production which never opened in New York.
‡Berlin married Ellin Mackay in 1926; the sensationalism arose out of her father's objection to her marrying a Jew. Millionaire Clarence Mackay was then president of the Postal Telegraph Co.

fun, though he tried to trick me with fancy steps, but I kept up with him. He was darling.

Frances Gershwin Godowsky, interview, 7 August 1990

HAROLD ARLEN
(1905–86)

Composer of the music to such songs as 'Stormy Weather', 'It's Only a Paper Moon', 'Over the Rainbow', 'Blues in the Night', 'The Man That Got Away', Arlen was a close friend of Gershwin's from the early thirties. He also collaborated with Ira Gershwin, most notably on the songs for the Judy Garland film, *A Star is Born*.

I believe that anyone who knows George's work, knows George. The humor, the satire, the playfulness of most of his melodic phrases were the natural expression of the man. But it might come as a surprise to those who know the Gershwin legend, of the man's excitement over his own work and his enthusiastic appreciation of every contribution he had to make, to learn that he also had a very eager enthusiasm and whole-hearted appreciation for what a great many of us were writing. At odd moments, at most unexpected times, he would be interested enough to tell us something nice about our work. And somehow or other, when George said something nice about my work, I had the grand feeling that he meant what he said and that it was not just a case of saying the right things. In fact, that was what characterized all of George's comments. There was a constructive insight in what he said which, in my case, helped me form a certain sense of musical values and aided me in becoming more directional. If, sometimes, we song writers aren't as nice to each other as we might be in judging our respective efforts if sometimes we look for flaws, instead of relaxing and abandoning ourselves to the mood and spirit of each other's music, let us recall how spontaneously George reacted to many of our songs as they were issued.

I know a certain young composer [Arlen himself] who was hailed in the lobby of Carnegie Hall one night, when George was the featured artist in the playing of his own composition with a symphony orchestra, with: 'Hey, kid, that new song of yours is a pip.' This from a man whose mind was supposed to be full of his own importance and the importance of the moment.

Harold Arlen, 'The Composer's Friend', *George Gershwin*, Merle Armitage, ed. (New York, 1938), p. 123

His eyes and mouth were sensitive; his chin was strong; his body, slender, wiry and rhythmic. In spite of the self-certainty of his own uniqueness, I always saw a questioning look – which to me meant humility. His greatness lay not only in his dynamic talent, drive and sureness, but in that questioning look.

. . . in Hollywood writing for films, we used to gather at parties and would inevitably wind up at the piano. I particularly noticed George's naturalness and the feeling-at-ease quality that he had. One night, terribly anxious about this, I cornered George and asked, 'George, you always seem so comfortable at the piano. Don't you ever get nervous?'

There was a moment of silence, then came the blunt truth. 'Of course – but I never let on.'

Harold Arlen, 'Introduction', Edward Jablonski, *George Gershwin* (New York, 1962), pp. 7–8

JEROME KERN
(1885–1945)

The second great influence on songwriter Gershwin was Kern (chronologically actually the first). He first became conscious of Kern at his aunt's wedding in 1914 (he was still in school and studying the piano), when he heard 'You're here and I'm here' (from *The Laughing Husband*) and 'They didn't believe me' (from *The Girl from Utah*). Gershwin regarded Kern's *Show Boat* as 'the finest light opera achievement in the history of American music.'

There never was anything puny or insignificant about the life, work or opinions of George Gershwin. He lived, labored, played, exulted and suffered with bigness and gusto . . .

There is not much that this unpracticed pen can add to the volumes already written in critical survey of George's work; yet one utterance may be recorded which came from the heart of the man and is illustrative of his stature. It came at the crossroads of his career, long after his dissatisfaction with Broadway musical comedy; even after he had unfolded his pinions and lifted himself into the realm of serious music: 'Do you think,' he asked with naïveté, 'that now I am capable of grand opera? Because, you know,' he continued, 'all I've got is a lot of talent and plenty of *chutzpah*.'

Jerome Kern, 'Tribute', *George Gershwin*, Merle Armitage, ed. (New York 1938), p. 120

ISAAC GOLDBERG

Something of the Hebrew–Christian morality clings to him still, especially where women are concerned. In their presence he is quite correct; for that matter, his conversation among men is masculine, but hardly Rabelaisian. He has been known, before his sister Frances married, to suggest in company that she pull her dresses down.

Isaac Goldberg, *George Gershwin* (New York, 1931), p. 27

BURTON LANE
(b. 1912)

A gifted composer, best known for his collaboration with E. Y. Harburg on the songs for *Finian's Rainbow* and Alan Jay Lerner for *On a Clear Day You Can See Forever*. Lane was an aspiring teenaged songwriter when he met Gershwin, who encouraged him and they remained friends for the rest of George Gershwin's life. Ira Gershwin and Lane collaborated on the film score, *Give a Girl a Break* in 1952.

I remember George as a person with tremendous energy. He would sit at the piano – you could feel electricity going through the room when he played. And he loved what he was doing. People used to say that if they would go to a party and George was there . . . he would play for four hours. I can understand that. He had such fun doing it and people had such fun listening to him. He was marvelous.

He was a tremendous pianist . . . He had such energy when he played. He could transpose into any key with the greatest of ease. He had total command of what he was doing. And one of the things separates George from everyone else in my mind are the greatest musical surprises that he would have in all of his music – unusual changes of keys, harmonic changes. He was one of the few composers who had a real sense of humor.

Burton Lane, conversation, 1986

NANETTE KUTNER

(1906–62)

Nanette Kutner was Gershwin's secretary from about the mid-1920s, and remained with him until the mid-1930s.

Meeting him proved a shock.

Here was no art pose, but blatant earthiness . . . he was alive; lusty, suntanned, athletic; wearing blue shirts, smoking black cigars.

. . . He had letters to write. And no one to write them. Autograph demands multiplied. The letters lay unanswered. It did not occur to him to have a secretary.

He finally purchased a portable typewriter, for a while playing with the keys, entranced.

Then we started on the letters. First, those in a chest of drawers near the bed. A note from Lady Diana Manners. One from Adele Astaire who puzzled him; her lovable outspoken breeziness remaining a mystery to his nature, self-conscious and studied.

Pictures come forward . . . When, exuberant, he danced the 'Black Bottom', to see if its steps fitted his rhythms; the time he argued, 'But everybody's got an ear!', refusing to credit my inherent lack; the rainy afternoon he thought was 'a swell day to work if I had an idea'; the morning his greeting exploded, 'I woke at three with a tune, even the title! I got right up and wrote it, like you read about! But now . . . it's not so hot!'*

---

*The song was 'I've Got Fidgety Feet' (*Funny Face*, 1926).

He leased an apartment, glaringly modern, a penthouse on Riverside Drive, away from the bulk of the family. There was a silver piano, and a bedroom that seemed all bed, the cover of light tan fur. Nothing out of place here, a punching bag in a room meant for games, a man wearing a white coat, who answered the door.

He still ran to the telephone himself . . .

His moods changed . . . Hurt surprise over a failure. Pacing the floor about it, shouting, *'They forget everything you've done when you've made one mistake!'*

Incredulous anger at [Florenz] Ziegfeld who held back royalties because *Show Girl* wasn't a hit. Dignified, dependable, he expected others to be the same. George Gershwin was probably the only man on Broadway who didn't have a lawyer.

He moved again to a duplex apartment on the east side. The enormous high-ceilinged living-room, fitting background for his newly acquired art collection, a modern and expensive assortment, wherein Gershwin's impression of his father audaciously stared at a Rousseau.

Nanette Kutner, 'Portrait in Our Time', *George Gershwin*, Merle Armitage, ed. (New York, 1938), pp. 237–42

ARTHUR SCHWARTZ
(1900–1984)

Composer of the haunting 'Dancing in the Dark', 'I See Your Face before Me', 'You and the Night and the Music' (all with his most frequent lyricist, Howard Dietz), Arthur Schwartz was also a film and theatre producer. He was especially productive and successful in the thirties, during which he and Dietz wrote songs for such revues as *The Band Wagon*, *At Home Abroad*, and others. He collaborated with Ira Gershwin in the songs for an unsuccessful show, *Park Avenue* (1946).

I first started thinking about George Gershwin when I was, I guess, a sophomore in college . . . At that time George was writing marvellous tunes – fresh, with a flavor that had never been heard before. I myself was *trying* to write tunes with no success at all and all my efforts would end with terrible frustration. I would find myself instead of playing the tunes I was trying to make up suddenly switching, with a fierce attitude, from my own into something that was currently Gershwin.

I didn't think when I got out of college that I had enough talent to risk a musical career . . . I studied law and practiced law. But my musical hopes were very furtive. I decided to meet him and then ask him to listen to some of my music. At that time I wrote a composition which I thought was absolutely marvelous. It was really a tribute to the *Rhapsody in Blue*. It was called 'I'm crazy about the Rhapsody in Blue' . . . Obviously I thought it was perfectly proper for me to use . . . certain phrases right out of the *Rhapsody* in a quotation which I regarded as rather affectionate. I had this appointment with George and he said, yes, he would listen to it. I was frightened out of my wits and the long introduction was ridiculous and as I was playing [it], I thought, How the dickens can I get out of this room? This is a foolish, preposterous idea, asking George to hear a corny composition about his own work. But . . . I had to go through with it and I did. I remember that the principle of the beginning of it was to quote a phrase right out of the *Rhapsody*, with lyrics, and it went something like this:

> Oh, wonderful, wonderful, Georgie –
> What you've done to me!
> Your classical, jazzical orgy,
> Won't let me be!

Well, that's as far as I got despite George's friendly insistence. I told him I was withdrawing the composition right then and there and I noticed he didn't quarrel with my decision . . . He changed the subject and I thought it was a merciful thing . . . He asked me to play some of my other melodies and he was very warm and very encouraging and gave me the feeling that perhaps I did have some talent and should persevere. I met him, of course, during our joint contemporary efforts and he was the most fascinating and talented man in the field . . .

He was both intuitive and he studied. I think he was more intuitive than educated . . .

I don't think that anyone who knew George well could accuse

him of being anything but charming, ingratiating and in every way acceptable as a companion no matter how he was occupied with himself. He had such charm and naïveté about his own work and himself that there was no feeling on the part of any of us composers or any of his friends who were constantly with him that his egocentricity was objectionable. Not at all. He did something that no other American composer had done – at the time [or] . . . since. He took the song form and enlarged it – that is, the contemporary song form, the idiom of his time, and wrote many compositions in extended form which nobody had since equalled . . . And to hear him sing in that piping voice of his was as . . . entertaining as to hear him play. He also tap danced; did you know that?

Arthur Schwartz, interview, 1961

KAY SWIFT

(b. 1897)

Composer, lyricist, pianist and writer, Kay Swift was a conservatory-trained musician and tended to look down on popular music – until she met Gershwin around 1926. Then, in collaboration with her husband, James Paul Warburg (of the prominent banking family), she wrote original, sophisticated songs. Warburg used the pen name of 'Paul James'. Among their creations were 'Can't We Be Friends?', 'Fine and Dandy' and 'Can This Be Love?'. Her concert compositions include a ballet, the song cycle *Reaching for the Brass Ring*, and *Man Have Pity on Man* (to a text by Ursula Vaughan Williams). Her relationship with Gershwin lasted about a decade, ending with his death shortly after he phoned her from California and said, 'I'm coming back for both of us.'

I thought theater music before I heard Gershwin was very predictable and bland. Maybe it wasn't, but it was my idea anyway, having been brought up in a classical background. And then I heard Gershwin music and I thought, Hey, here's something different and new! . . . When I met him nothing let me down. He played wonderfully and he was exactly like his music in person. It was a curious thing – I think most of us fail to hide in our work; it was especially true of George, who was exactly like his work. Oh, it was so stimulating [to hear him play]. I've seen very old people and kids, and people that were very stiffo about popular music or playing music for shows, and they rushed to the piano and hung over it . . . they were so stimulated that some of them were even starting to do a dance. People became unselfconscious; that was the great thing he did for people – one of the great things. He made them forget themselves entirely and just think about the music, which was such an escape, like a trip to another country. They all felt it because they made him play so long. If he played at a party, he wouldn't play for fifteen minutes; he'd sit there for an hour. I've seen him play for an hour-and-a-quarter, and [an] hour-and-a-half, enjoying himself and everyone saying, 'Go on! More, more!'

George felt, very strongly, that there were a lot of shallow and uninteresting materials at the top of the mind of every composer. So he always used to say, 'Play that out,' or, 'Write it out till you get past it, because underneath are the good things and, moreover . . . very often the music on top is apt to be tragic, very sad, very wistful and wandering.'

I said, 'Why do you suppose that is?'

'Oh,' [George said] 'I think if a composer felt all that happy, he could think of better things to do than hang over a hot piano.'

He was rather typically of New York. I think he might have had some different, perhaps superficial characteristics had he come from Chicago, San Francisco, or wherever. He was busy, quick and moved fast, which, I think, means New York. And he had curiosity, was always going on a new tack – I think that's New Yorkish.

I think he knew how good he was. He would have been a jackass not to, after all, wouldn't he? But he didn't take himself seriously as a person, not a bit. He wasn't pompous. I think he took his music seriously and I think he thought of it as something he had to do and looked at it almost reverently because it was that good. So it made him careful. He doesn't sound careful, he sounds so easy. He put just as much into writing a song as writing *An American in Paris* or any of the other pieces, because it was important and he knew it.

He was like an element – like wind or rain or sun, spring or winter.
He was that basic – and important accordingly.

Kay Swift, *Forever Gershwin*, WCNB–TV, Boston 3 May 1974

IRA GERSHWIN

Sibling rivalry aside, Ira Gershwin was undoubtedly one
of his brother's most devoted admirers. Many of the years
after Gershwin's death were devoted to answering 'fan'
letters (some unconsciously intended for George though
addressed to Ira), preserving and attending to Gershwin-
iana and its placement in the Gershwin Archive at the
Library of Congress, Washington, DC. He spent a good
part of his later years carefully annotating it – manuscripts,
letters, etc., – before depositing it in the Archive. After
the failure of his last Broadway show, *Park Avenue*, in
1946, Ira Gershwin returned to his home in Beverly Hills
(in a house adjacent to the one in which they had lived
during his brother's last year). From there he collaborated
on a handful of films, *The Shocking Miss Pilgrim* (1947),
with a posthumous George Gershwin score, arranged with
the assistance of Kay Swift; *The Barkleys of Broadway*, with
music by Harry Warren, and the interpolation of 'They
can't take that away from me'; *Give a Girl a Break*, music
by Burton Lane; the Judy Garland hit, *A Star is Born*,
music by Harold Arlen; and *A Country Girl*, also with
Arlen. He released a couple of unpublished Gershwin
songs for a film quite properly entitled *Kiss Me, Stupid* in
1964. He made some contribution to the filming of the
Gershwin cornucopia, *An American in Paris* (1951). After
The Country Girl he devoted the bulk of his time to
nurturing his brother's career and works until his own
death in 1983. His one book, *Lyrics on Several Occasions*
(1959), is a charming collection of words and words upon
words, with many apportioned to George Gershwin.

From Gershwin emanated a new American music not written with the
ruthlessness of one who strives to demolish established rules, but based
on a new native gusto and wit and awareness. His was a modernity

that reflected the civilization we live in as excitingly as the headline
in today's newspaper.

(1938)
I always felt that if George hadn't been my brother and pushed me
into lyric writing, I'd have been contented to be a bookkeeper.

Edward Jablonski, Lawrence D. Stewart, *The Gershwin Years* (New York,
1958), p. 310

Something, even much, has been made of George's musical ambiv-
alence. That is, on the one hand he wrote popular songs and Broadway
and Hollywood scores – and on the other, concert works like Concerto
in F and *An American in Paris*. However, it was not a matter of
leading a double musical life. He was just as demanding of his
talent when writing an opening for a revue as when composing and
orchestrating his opera, *Porgy and Bess*. It was all one to him. And
the longevity of the natural-born oneness is quite amazing.

Foreword, *The George and Ira Gershwin Song-book* (New York, 1960),
pp. ix-x

Though George was 18 months or so younger than I, I felt he could
do anything. As a matter of fact, his first term in high school he came
back one day and said, 'Oh, I played in the assembly today,' just
casually. The principal asked: Can anybody play the piano and George
raised his hand and he played the marches for [his classmates] to come
in. So I always felt that anything he tried to do, he would be successful
at. So when I began writing songs with him, he was a celebrity . . .
I was just beginning and didn't want to trade on his name even though
he was my younger brother. So I took a pseudonym of my brother
Arthur and my sister Frances. I became 'Arthur Francis' for several
years. But the point was I didn't want to impinge on George's
reputation . . . But later on I felt I was pretty well known. I had
written with many other song writers by that time.* Also I found out
that there was an Arthur Francis in the British Performing Rights
Society. So there was another reason for discarding 'Arthur Francis',
and becoming Ira Gershwin.

*1924, the year of their first major collaboration on *Lady, be Good!*; after this there was no
more Arthur Francis in the US.

. . . mostly I wrote to tunes. George would say, 'Here's a good tune for such and such a spot. I would stay up nights. I would learn it very quickly, memorize the tune; sometimes I'd get a lead sheet, also, if I weren't sure. Then I'd work and work on it, starting at midnight, sometimes at two in the morning and work till six or seven in the morning. Then I'd submit the idea to him . . .

Later on, we worked together much more than that. I remember when we did the films in '36 and '37, we discussed an idea – I might have a title and he would start setting it and we'd say that's a pretty good start and we'd work up, together, the tune and the lyric.

One very successful song that way was when George came home from a party one night. I was reading and I said, 'George, I got an idea for Astaire. How do you like "A foggy day in London town?" ' [This was for a film, A *Damsel in Distress*]. He said, 'That sounds good.' In half an hour we finished the refrain. But we were both hot for the moment for that situation. Of course, then we had to do the verse later and that took much more time. We were very careful with verses, we always wanted to make them as good as refrains. Of course, nobody cares about verses anymore. But we spent as much time on verses as we did refrains. [About this verse] I said to George, 'I hear a sort of Irish effect.' And he knew immediately what I meant. [In his book Ira Gershwin explained further: '. . . he sensed instantly the degree of wistful loneliness.']

Ira Gershwin, interview with Stuart Triff, 8 May 1968

Hollywood didn't want him really. Our agent called us here in New York and said, 'They think George is too highbrow. Can't he write a few words and explain to them?' So George sent a wire which said simply, 'I am not highbrow and never have been. I have written many successful songs in the past and hope to write many more.'

Whenever I did a show with George, I always felt as if I'd earned a year off. I was never very energetic. George had all the energy. He'd know exactly what I had in mind.

New York Daily News, 27 May 1953

Sometime in the middle twenties my brother and I spent three weeks or so with librettist Herbert Fields on a musical to be called *The Big*

Charade. I forget now why this project was dropped. Anyhow, we did some work on it, including a pseudo-medieval march called 'Trumpets of Belgravia'. Years later, when *Of Thee I Sing* was being written, my brother was dissatisfied with several starts he had made for the opening – a political campaign marching theme which inevitably had to be titled 'Wintergreen for President'. One day, out of the blue, I found myself humming these seven syllables to the exact rhythm and tune of the cast-behind 'Trumpets of Belgravia/Sing ta-ra, ta-ra, ta-ra . . .' When I suggested this tune to its composer, his approval was non-verbal but physical. He immediately went to the piano and 'Trumpets of Belgravia' became the serendipitous start of 'Wintergreen for President'.

Ira Gershwin, *Lyrics on Several Occasions* (New York, 1959), p. 107

'*Extra Long Verses*'. When 'By Strauss' was being prepared for sheet-music publication, my brother received a letter from a concerned young woman in the editing department. She wrote that the verse was 'unusually long' and 'would take up at least three pages . . . Is there anything you can suggest that would help us to get the number out in the usual amount of pages?' (usually two.) On 12/4/36 my brother wrote:

Dear Selma,

I am very sorry that the verse to BY STRAUSS is so long that it requires perhaps an extra page in the publication copy, but then it's always been my policy to give the public a lot for their money; and I think it would be a good idea to put on the title page – 'This song has an extra long verse so you are getting more notes per penny than in any other song this season.' . . . And even if the song doesn't even sell I would like my grandchildren (if I ever have any) to see the trouble that their grand-daddy took with verses. In other words, dear Selma, I would like the song printed as I wrote it, with no commas left out.

Love and kisses,
GEORGE

Lyrics on Several Occasions, p. 171

. . . the only instance wherein DuBose tried working to a tune [was for 'I got plenty o' nuthin"]. All his fine and poetic lyrics were set to music by George with scarcely a syllable being changed – an aspect of the composer's versatility not generally recognized. These many years . . . and I can still shake my head in wonder at the reservoir of musical inventiveness, resourcefulness, and craftsmanship George could dip into. And no fraternal entracement, my wonderment. He takes two simple quatrains of DuBose's, studies the lines, and in a little while a lullaby called 'Summertime' emerges – delicate and wistful, yet destined to be sung over and over again. Out of the libretto's dialogue he takes Bess's straight, unrhymed speech which starts: 'What do you want wid Bess? She's gettin' old now,' and it becomes a rhythmic aria; then he superimposes Crown's lines, 'What I wants wid other woman? I gots a woman,' and now is heard at once a moving and exultant duet. Not a syllable of DuBose's poignant 'My Man's Gone Now' is changed as the composer sets it to waltz time, adds the widow's heartrending wail between stanzas, and climaxes the tragic lament with an ascending glissando – resulting in one of the most memorable moments in the American musical theater.

Lyrics on Several Occasions, pp. 360–61

I wish some of those who think they knew him, wouldn't write stories about him. As great a composer as he was, George was never brassy, never hard to get along with. He was shy, reserved, a sweet guy. His real friends, of which there were many, knew him this way, too.

'About Ira', *Music Business*, October 1946, p. 29

KAY HALLE

(b. *c* 1900)

Author Kay Halle met Gershwin in Cleveland during his 1934 cross-country tour with an orchestra conducted by Charles Previn. She served as intermission commentator for the Cleveland Orchestra's radio broadcasts. After re-settling in New York she saw a good deal of Gershwin. She is the author of *Irrepressible Churchill*.

His brother, Ira, whose lyrics heightened the impact of George's music, also served as a counterbalance to the fun-loving life of his adored brother. They were close, and throughout most of their creative lives, lived in adjoining apartments on Riverside Drive.

George's 72nd Street apartment, with its pale green panelled walls and comfortable furniture, was alive with a cross-section of his talented friends. There might be the philosopher–architect Buckminster Fuller . . . A frequent guest was Fred Astaire. Composers Dick Rodgers, Jerome Kern, Irving Berlin, with a mix of English nobility and the star actors and actresses of the moment, were also regulars at these gatherings. There were sure to be some artists among the guests, as George had become deeply interested in painting. Isamu Noguchi, the sculptor . . . was among the favored.

There was a piano or two in each room – or so it seemed – but it was on his Hammond organ that George tested each new composition for its fuller orchestral effect . . .

Most enjoyable were George's cozy luncheons of six to eight guests, with his fox terrier, Tony, always at his side. George was fascinated by new inventions, and surprisingly knowledgeable about scientific matters. I remember one occasion when he asked his butler to go out and bring back six copies of *Popular Mechanics*, his favorite magazine – one for each guest.

His appetite for innovation was insatiable. One evening, upon learning that 'Stuff' Smith, the phenomenal 'hot' violinist, was performing with his band at the Onyx club at 53rd Street in New York, we took off to hear them. Soon after a waiter had placed us at our table 'Stuff' and his orchestra went into a maze of intriguing and intricate convolutions of sounds and rhythms. When they finished, 'Stuff' came over to greet a puzzled George, who asked him what they had been playing. 'Why, Mr Gershwin,' he chuckled, 'don't you recognize "I Got Rhythm"?'

. . . the event that moved George most in his 38 years was an invitation from his great admirer, President Roosevelt, to come with me to a New Year's party at the White House on Dec. 29, 1934. As we reached the entrance hall leading to the East Room, George's joy and excitement were so unbounded that he shot away from the receiving line to stand under the glittering chandelier, joyfully crying out, 'If only my father could see me now!'

Kay Halle, 'The Time of His Life', *Washington Post*, 5 February 1978, pp. F5–F6

OSCAR LEVANT

The stories about George Gershwin and his totally confident opinion about himself are many. Not too well known is the one about the time he took a taxi uptown to see a Columbia football game. The driver wove an arabesque between the supports of the then elevated railroad. George leaned over and tapped him on the shoulder. 'For God's sake, man,' he remonstrated, 'drive carefully! You've got Gershwin in the car!'

George once remarked, after a Don Quixote tilt with a blond windmill in the form of a charming girl, 'She has a little love for everyone and not a great deal for anybody.'

Whether true of the girl or not, I feel that George had unconsciously mirrored himself in these words.

Oscar Levant, *A Smattering of Ignorance* (New York, 1941), pp. 150, 201

IRVING BERLIN

(1888–1989)

One of the two great early influences on Gershwin, Berlin was his lifelong friend and admirer. When, early in his career, Gershwin applied for a job as Berlin's musical secretary (Berlin could not read music), he was rejected. Berlin explained that Gershwin's own talent was too original and distinguished to be subservient to another's. Berlin was a forthright, often blunt, conversationalist; his terse, to the point remarks reveal him not only as a man of a few words but also of insight.

George Gershwin is the only song writer I know who became a composer.

Irving Berlin, in conversation with the editor, *c.* 1961

VI

The Creation of *Porgy and Bess*

One afternoon in the autumn of 1926 Gershwin showed his secretary, Nanette Kutner, 'a thin book, declaring, "Some day I'll make an opera out of it." The book, just published, was titled *Porgy*.' At the time Gershwin was occupied with rehearsals for *Oh, Kay!* which starred Gertrude Lawrence. As opening night approached the work grew more hectic, and the composer spent long hours in the theatre. After an especially long session, he decided to read himself to sleep with a book given him by his friends Emily and Lou Paley. Instead of sleeping Gershwin finished the novel, went to his desk just before dawn to write to the author, DuBose Heyward, about converting the novel about black fishermen in Charleston, South Carolina, into an opera. Heyward was delighted but only then learned that for the past seven months, his wife, Dorothy, had been using the novel as the basis for a play. Unruffled, Gershwin told the Heywards that before he attempted the opera, he would require more study of the form and other musical technicalities. There the project rested for a half dozen years, and Gershwin went on to other things: several musicals, an early film, *An American in Paris*, the Piano Preludes. The Heywards scored a great success with their dramatized *Porgy* in 1927; Heyward continued writing novels, and screenplays (such as Pearl Buck's *The Good Earth*). Then in an economically lean period in his life, in the depths of the Depression, he received a second, unexpected and welcome letter from Gershwin, who was restless and characteristically eager to be doing something after the opening of *Of Thee I Sing* and the première of his *Second Rhapsody*. He needed the activity and Heyward needed the money (unfortunately for him the project would stretch over a greater period of time than he expected because of Gershwin's other activities, including a radio show that helped finance his operatic ambitions).

The *Porgy and Bess* collaboration was doubly unique: Gershwin and Heyward rarely saw one another – most of their work was accomplished by mail. Secondly, it was undoubtedly one of the most ego-free collaborations in the history of the American theatre, one of deep mutual respect, of temperaments in unusual harmonic convergence. There is no doubt that George Gershwin, though the younger member of the team (thirteen years younger), was definitely the first among equals. When the opera was eventually begun, Ira Gershwin was collaborating with others; later, at Heyward's suggestion, he was brought into the project. When, in March of 1932, Heyward heard from Gershwin, his reply set the genteel, self-effacing tone of their collaboration.

DUBOSE HEYWARD

(1885–1940)

Poet, author and folklorist, Heyward collaborated as a playwright with his wife, Dorothy Kuhn Heyward. Her adaptation of *Porgy* was used by Heyward as the source of *Porgy and Bess*. Their last collaboration was *Mamba's Daughters*, produced the year of Heyward's death. Early in 1937 Gershwin, writing from Beverly Hills, suggested that he and Heyward collaborate on another opera.

My first impression of my collaborator remains with me and is singularly vivid. A young man of enormous physical and emotional vitality, who possessed the faculty of seeing himself quite impersonally and realistically, and who knew exactly what he wanted and where he was going. This characteristic put him beyond both modesty and conceit. About himself he would merely mention certain facts, aspirations, failings . . .

We discussed *Porgy*. He said that it would not matter about the dramatic production (in 1927), as it would be a number of years before he would be prepared technically to compose an opera. At the time he had numerous Broadway successes to his credit, and his *Rhapsody in Blue* . . . had placed him in the front rank of American composers. It was extraordinary, I thought, in view of a success that might have dazzled any man, he could appraise his talent with such complete detachment.

DuBose Heyward, 'Porgy and Bess Return on Wings of Song', *Stage Magazine*, October 1935, pp. 25–8

I want to tell you again how pleased I am that you have returned to your original idea of doing a musical setting of Porgy. I would be tremendously interested in working on the book with you. I have some new material that might be introduced, and once I get your ideas as to the general form suitable for the musical version, I am sure that I could do you a satisfactory story. As to the lyrics, I am not so sure until I know more definitely what you have in mind. Perhaps your brother Ira would want to do them, Or maybe we could do them together. At any rate I want you to feel that I would be happy to do what you want me to, and at the same time you must feel entirely free to use anyone else that you might wish.

DuBose Heyward, letter to George Gershwin, 12 April 1932

> Heyward's expectations, it turned out, were a bit premature. Though he set the musicalization of *Porgy* in motion, Gershwin informed Heyward in his next letter that he could not begin work on the opera until January 1933. In fact, he did not begin composing until late February 1934 because of other commitments. Once the work began he devoted himself to it unlike any other composition.

IRA GERSHWIN

Porgy and Bess, his most ambitious work, was composed in eleven months and he did the orchestration in nine; during this period he also did a good deal of broadcasting. Although most of the opera was done in New York, parts were written in Charleston's Folly Beach, in Westchester (NY), in Palm Beach, in Fire Island and in the Adirondacks.

Ira Gershwin, 'My Brother', *George Gershwin*, Merle Armitage, ed. (New York, 1938), p. 22

> During this period, and before he began composing, the

Gershwins collaborated on two musicals, *Pardon My English* and *Let 'em Eat Cake*, neither of which was successful, despite exceptional scores. There was also an incident that might have caused a complete change of plans. Vaudeville star Al Jolson came on the scene.

DUBOSE HEYWARD

I cannot see brother Jolson as Porgy, but I have heard that he was casting about for something more artistic than his usual Sonny Boy line . . .

Of course, this does not shake me in my desire to work with you on the story, only it reminds me that I evidently have an asset in Porgy, and in these trying times that has to be considered. Therefore, before I turn this down flat, I think that we should execute the customary agreement with your producer, with whom, I presume, you have been already discussing the matter.

DuBose Heyward, letter to Gershwin, 3 September 1932

GEORGE GERSHWIN

I think it is very interesting that Al Jolson would like to play the part of Porgy, but I really don't know how he would be in it. Of course, he is a very big star, who certainly knows how to put over a song, and it might mean more to you financially if he should do it – provided that the rest of the production is well done. The sort of thing that I should have in mind for PORGY is a much more serious thing than Jolson could ever do.

Of course I would not attempt to write music to your play until I had all the themes and musical devices worked out for such an undertaking. It would be more a labor of love than anything else . . . I have not planned with any producers yet as I should like to write the work first and then see who would be the best one to do it . . .

George Gershwin, letter to DuBose Heyward, 9 September 1932

Left Gershwin as a teenager, *c.* 1914

Right Wedding picture of Morris and Rose Bruskin Gershwin, *c.* 1895

Top Gershwin's birthplace, Brooklyn, NY

Left Frances Gershwin

Right Charles Hambitzer

Top Fred and Adele Astaire, who starred in *Lady, be Good!*, 1924,
and *Funny Face*, 1927

Left Tin Pan Alley around the time Gershwin worked as a pianist for the
Jerome H. Remick Company, 24 West 28th Street

Right Gershwin in 1918

Top At his desk at the T. B. Harms Co., *c.* February 1918

Lyricist Irving Caesar

Top left Gershwin and his first published 'serious' composition

Top right New York *Tribune*, 4 January 1924

Successful songwriter with the man (to Gershwin's right) responsible, Al Jolson. Jolson's performance of the song in his revue *Sinbad*, and his best-selling recording of Gershwin and Irving Caesar's 'Swanee', made Gershwin a celebrated Tin Pan Alley composer

Top left Gershwin in the early 1930s

Top right In a radio studio with his early
musical hero, Jerome Kern

Right Gertrude Lawrence
and Gershwin, 1926

Top Rare family photograph, *c.* 1930/31: George, Arthur, Rose, Morris and Ira. Frankie Gershwin had by this time married Leopold Godowsky, Jr, and was living in Rochester, NY, base of Eastman Kodak, for whom Leopold had co-invented Kodachrome, a colour process.

Studying the score of the Concerto in F with conductor Walter Damrosch, 1925

Top left At the Auteuil racetrack, Paris, April 1926; while staying with Mabel and Robert Schirmer he conceived the idea for a new work he planned to call *An American in Paris*

Top right Jerome Kern photographed by George Gershwin

Oscar Levant photographed by George Gershwin

Top At work in the living room at 1019 North Roxbury Drive,
Beverly Hills, early 1937

Left George and Ira around the time of *Lady, be Good!* 1924

Right Kay Swift

Top left Irving Berlin photographed by George Gershwin in 1936

Top right Orchestrating *Porgy and Bess*, Palm Beach, Florida

DuBose Heyward and Ira Gershwin, librettist lyricist and lyricist of
Porgy and Bess, 1935

Top As host of his radio show, 'Music by Gershwin', 1934

Mabel Schirmer, *c.* 1935, photographed by George Gershwin

Top While in Boston for the try-out of *Porgy and Bess*, the collaborators exchanged signed photographs, September 1935

Opening night curtain call: Georgette Harvey, Ruby Elzy, Todd Duncan, Anne Brown, Rouben Mamoulian (the director), Gershwin, Heyward (partly hidden), Warren Coleman and others

Top left Programme cover for Whiteman's concert

Top right Completing his watercolour 'Me', April 1929

Gershwin and Botkin. To Gershwin's right is Picasso's 'The Absinthe Drinker';
Botkin's 'Ten Miles from Charleston' is on the wall directly behind him. It
was done during their stay on Folly Island, South Carolina, June/July 1934

Top left Self-portrait in a chequered sweater, 1936

Top right With his oil portrait of Arnold Schoenberg, Beverly Hills, 1937

On the set of *Shall We Dance*, 1936. Standing: dance director Hermes Pan, director Mark Sandrich, Ira Gershwin, musical director Nat Shilkret. Stars Fred Astaire and Ginger Rogers are seated next to Gershwin

Top French starlet Simone Simon, with whom Gershwin had a brief romance

Gershwin with Paulette Goddard, then wife of Charles Chaplin

Top right The last known
photograph, RKO-Radio
Pictures convention, 16 June
1937, less than a month before
his death

Above Gershwin, *c.* 1925

Right During 1925 Gershwin
worked almost simultaneously on
the Concerto in F, *Tell Me More*,
Tip-toes and *Sound of the Flame*.
Though he could work with
people around, he sometimes
sought a little quiet by slipping
off to rooms he had taken in the
nearby Whitehall Hotel on
Broadway and 100th Street

DUBOSE HEYWARD

Miss Wood of the Century Play Company writes that Jolson has been hot on her trail for the Porgy book, and that in a 'phone conversation with you, she was advised by you that his use of the story for his sort of musical play would not necessarily kill it for an eventual opera.*

As a matter of fact, upon my return here after my talk with you I learned of circumstances that have put me in a fairly tight spot financially. . . . Please let me tell you that I think your attitude in this matter is simply splendid. It makes me all the more eager to work with you some day, some time, before we wake up and find ourselves in our dotage.

DuBose Heyward, letter to Gershwin, 17 October 1932

> Jolson gave up when Kern and Hammerstein decided to leave for England to work on a new musical, *Three Sisters*. In November 1933 Heyward began working on the opera and mailing his work to Gershwin, who had not yet begun writing. In October, he and Heyward signed a contract with the Theatre Guild to do their opera. In December, while in Florida preparing for his cross-country tour, Gershwin composed the *Variations on 'I Got Rhythm'* and a sketch for 'Summertime', the opera's first song. Finally, on 26 February 1934, he told Heyward, 'I have begun composing music for the First Act and I am starting with the songs and spirituals first.'

DUBOSE HEYWARD

I have been hearing you on the radio, and the reception was so good it seemed as though you were in the room. In fact the illusion was so perfect I could hardly keep from shouting at you, 'Swell show, George, but what the hell is the news about PORGY!!!!' You have managed to give it a charming informality, and, in spite of the brevity, a definite impress of your personality. I am naturally disappointed that you have

---

*Neither Gershwin nor Heyward were aware of Jolson's desire to have Jerome Kern and Oscar Hammerstein to do the score. Their *Show Boat* had come close to being an opera.

tied yourself up so long in New York. I believe that if you had gotten down for a reasonably long stay and gotten deep into the sources here you would have done a bigger job. I am not criticizing your decision. I know well what an enormously advantageous arrangement the radio is, and I know, also, how this tour* of yours and the broadcasts are rolling up publicity that will be good business for us when the show opens, only I am disappointed.

DuBose Heyward, letter to Gershwin, 2 March 1934

> Two weeks after the final broadcast of 'Music by Gershwin' on 31 March 1934, Gershwin accompanied by his artist cousin Henry Botkin boarded a train for Charleston, South Carolina. They were followed by Gershwin's factotum, Paul Mueller, in an automobile carrying odds and ends, including painting equipment. Gershwin rented a cottage on Folly Beach, on a barrier island, about twenty miles south-east of Charleston, where he and Botkin would spend six weeks. The Heywards joined them soon after they had settled in. Gershwin found the place 'primitive' and was surprised by its lack of comfort: 'Imagine,' he wrote his mother, 'there's not *one* telephone on the island – public or private.'

HENRY BOTKIN

In the Folly Island retreat, the appointments were not of Waldorf Astoria level. Gershwin had a crudely decorated room, furnished with a primitive iron bed, a small washbasin and an old fashioned upright piano imported from Charleston.

Clothes were hung from hooks and shoes and baggage stored under the bed. Drinking water was brought in from Charleston in five gallon crocks.

Sidney Jerome, 'Porgy, Botkin and Bess', *Village Chatter*, June/July 1947, p. 20

---

*From 14 January to 10 February 1934, Gershwin toured with an orchestra giving twenty-eight concerts in as many cities in the US and one in Canada.

KAY HALLE

While composing his *Porgy and Bess*, I would receive ecstatic letters from Folly Beach . . . where . . . he was immersing himself in plantation and Southern lifestyles. It was the spirituals that captivated him most on his visits to the churches – especially the ones where the Holy Rollers were singing 'Dr Jesus, reach down from Heaven and place a bellyband of love around me.'*

Kay Halle, 'The Time of His Life', *Washington Post*, 5 February 1978, pp. F5–F6

DUBOSE HEYWARD

The Gullah Negro prides himself on what he calls 'shouting'. This is a complicated rhythmic pattern beaten out by feet and hands as an accompaniment to the spirituals, and is indubitably an African survival. I shall never forget the night when, at a Negro meeting on a remote sea-island, George started 'shouting' with them. And eventually to their huge delight, stole the show from their champion 'shouter'. I think that he is probably the only white man in America who could have done it.

Dubose Heyward, 'Porgy and Bess Return on Wings of Song', *Stage Magazine*, October 1935, pp. 25–8

MRS JOSEPH I. WARING

He was very close to the Heywards; that's how I met him. We were living on Sullivan's Island; they at Folly. George did love it here . . . He was very happy. He used to take off his shirt and walk up and down the beach, and in the evenings we would walk and sing spirituals. He loved to walk on the beach; he got burned nearly black because he loved the sun. DuBose would take him to the colored churches and schools. Someone told me of his playing in a colored school with a big picture of Robert E. Lee above him. He got around.

Mrs Joseph I. Waring, reminiscences, courtesy of Frances Gershwin Godowsky, 1979

*A reference to the spiritual which Gershwin uses as 'Oh, Doctor Jesus'.

DUBOSE HEYWARD

Another night as we were about to enter a dilapidated cabin that had been taken as a meeting house by a group of Negro Holy Rollers, George caught my arm and held me. The sound that had arrested him was one to which, through long familiarity, I attached no special importance. But now, listening to it with him, and noticing his excitement, I began to catch its extraordinary quality. It consisted of perhaps a dozen voices raised in loud rhythmic prayer. The odd thing about it was that while each had started at a different time, upon a different theme, they formed a clearly defined rhythmic pattern, and that this, with the actual words lost, and the inevitable pounding of the rhythm, produced an effect almost terrifying in its primitive intensity. Inspired by the extraordinary effect, George wrote six simultaneous prayers producing a terrifying invocation to God in the face of a hurricane.

Dubose Heyward, 'Porgy and Bess Return on Wings of Song', *Stage Magazine*, October 1935, pp. 25–8

KAY HALLE

In one letter he wrote, 'I am fascinated by the beaches, the black bambinos, the crabs and turtles with 160 egg nests. There is music in the turtles, in the rhythm of the laying of their eggs, first one, then two, then one and two eggs at a time . . .' Then, changing the subject, he went on, 'Your letter was like a drink to a thirsty man . . . so anxious was I to hear what my Yankee friends are up to, because they are still talking about the war – the Civil War – down here . . .'

George had become so deeply identified with the black life around Folly Beach and Charleston that he found the whites 'more unemotional, dull and drab in comparison'.

Kay Halle, 'The Time of His Life', *Washington Post*, 5 February 1978, p. F5.

MRS JOSEPH I. WARING

One evening we got the Society for the Preservation of Spirituals together. It was in the summer. And that was fine, except the Society for the Preservation of Spirituals didn't sing very long, because George began to play. Everybody said, 'Play this. Play that.' We had a glorious evening, listening to George play the piano, rather than singing, as we should have been doing for him.

Mrs Joseph I. Waring, reminiscences, courtesy of Frances Gershwin Godowsky

HENRY BOTKIN

Many, many eerie sand crabs looking very much like glass spiders, crawled around the cottage. They were the color of beach sand; nature's own way of camouflaging them. Droves of bugs and insects fly against the screen and the noisy crickets drove George to distraction, keeping him awake at nights.

Sidney Jerome, 'Porgy, Botkin and Bess', *Village Chatter*, June/July 1947, p. 20

ASHLEY COOPER

As a young reporter for the *News & Courier*, I went to Folly to interview him. He wasn't in the cottage, but I found him speeding along the beach in an open car, grinning like a kid. I waved him down and told him I was a reporter.

'Get in and ride, and you can ask me questions', said he. But he was much too excited to pay very close attention to my questions. Remember, Gershwin was a New York City man and had spent almost his entire life there. He had never seen anything like Folly Beach. To him Folly was nature in the raw, back to the wilderness. It fascinated him, and he loved it.

'I've never ridden on a beach before', he beamed. 'It's exciting, eh?'
Then he took me to the cottage where he was staying, and he and

I sampled some Hell Hole Swamp corn Whiskey, a Prohibition product. And Gershwin talked about music.

'I've never lived in such a back-to-nature place', he said . . . At home, I get up about noon. Here, I get up at 7.00 – well, at 7.30 anyway.'

He couldn't talk about music very long without wanting to play a piano. There was an old upright in the cottage on which he had been composing, and he sat down at it and said, 'Here's a good one.'

Then he grinned and batted out the first couple of lines of his great hit, 'I got rhythm'. Then he played 'The last roundup', singing with it.* Although I have always had a voice which has been known to frighten crows, I joined in. As for George, he wasn't Bing Crosby, either. But before you knew it, two black servants, back in the kitchen, were beating time. And George was playing. And he and I were singing.

He paused for a minute to apologize for his playing – which, just the same, was superb. He held up the taped index finger of his right hand and explained that he had cut it trying to make a hole in one of his suitcase straps.

It was well after dark when I finally left. By that time, 30 or 40 people – mostly servants from nearby cottages – were sitting out front. George kept playing, and the people out front were swaying to the music. 'Don't know who that man is playing the piano', said one of the listeners, 'But that man can really play!'

Ashley Cooper, *Charleston News & Courier*, courtesy of Frances Gershwin Godowsky

> Back in New York by July 21, Gershwin had little time for more work on *Porgy and Bess*, though he began the orchestration of scene 2 of the first Act in September. On the 30th the half hour 'Music by Gershwin' was broadcast with his friend (and recent collaborator with Ira), Harold Arlen, as guest. After the final broadcast on 23 December 1934, he turned to the orchestration of his opera in earnest.

---

*Not a Gershwin song; words and music are by Billy Hill.

MABEL SCHIRMER

(b. 1897)

A lifelong friend, Mabel Pleshette Schirmer knew Gershwin from his teens when her uncle, songwriter Herman
Paley, brought Gershwin to their home in Manhattan.
Gershwin introduced Mabel Pleshette to Charles Hambitzer, from whom she took piano lessons.

George did not like to be alone, not even when he was working. In
1935 I lived nearby, on East Seventy-Eighth Street. Often he would
call me in the morning and invite me to lunch. After lunch he would
settle in his workroom and, while I did petit point, he would work.
It must have been on the orchestrations – I don't recall his playing
the piano very often. After he'd finish for the day we'd go for a walk
in Central Park. He was a very strenuous walker!

Edward Jablonski, *Gershwin* (New York, 1987), p. 285

ROUBEN MAMOULIAN

George was particularly keen to orchestrate the score all by himself.
He worked very long and hard at it. He wrote me in a letter, 'I am
orchestrating the opera at the present time and have about five months'
work left. It is really a tremendous task scoring three hours of music.'
It was and he did it. (And his was such a beautiful-looking manuscript!)

Rouben Mamoulian, 'I Remember', *George Gershwin*, Merle Armitage, ed.
(New York, 1938), pp. 48–9

EVA JESSYE

(b. 1895)

Choral director of *Porgy and Bess*, Eva Jessye had earlier
been choral director of Virgil Thomson's all-black opera,
Four Saints in Three Acts.

George didn't interfere during rehearsals; he let us do what we knew

how to do. A very sad-looking man around the mouth. I remember
he loved peanuts, and he was always cracking them and eating them
during the times he'd come to watch us . . .

He invited me up to his penthouse on 72nd Street. I remember a
glassed-in flower conservatory and the three Steinways in the apartment, two downstairs for two-piano work, and one upstairs. But the
first thing I noticed was a long table with several copyists busily
working on the score of *Porgy and Bess*.

Robert Kimball and Alfred Simon, *The Gershwins* (New York, 1973), p. 184

ROUBEN MAMOULIAN

The first day of rehearsing a play is always difficult. It is like breaking
mountains of ice. The end of it leaves one completely exhausted and
usually a little depressed . . . That's the way I felt after the first day
of *Porgy and Bess*. I lay in my bed . . . indulging in rather melancholy
and misanthropic thoughts. Suddenly the phone rang and George
Gershwin was announced. This delighted me as I felt in need of
encouragement and kind words. I picked up the receiver and said
'Hello' with eager anticipation. George's voice came glowing with
enthusiasm: 'Rouben, I couldn't help calling you . . . I just *had* to
call you and tell you how I feel. I am so thrilled and delighted over
the rehearsal today.' (My heart started warming up and I already
began to feel better!) 'Of course,' he went on, 'I always knew that
Porgy and Bess was wonderful, but I never thought I'd feel the way I
feel now. I tell you, after listening to that rehearsal today, I think the
music is so marvelous – I really don't believe I wrote it!'

Rouben Mamoulian, 'I Remember', *George Gershwin*, Merle Armitage, ed.
(New York, 1938), p. 51

TODD DUNCAN
(b. 1903)

Teacher and recitalist: when Gershwin chose him for the
role of 'Porgy', Todd Duncan was teaching voice at
Howard University, Washington, DC. He appeared in

the film *Cabin in the Sky* (1940), and in the musical play
Lost in the Stars (1949), an adaptation of Alan Paton's
novel, *Cry, the Beloved Country* by Kurt Weill and
Maxwell Anderson.

It was my good fortune to have him accompany me in his own songs
under every conceivable condition . . . A performance with George
Gershwin was a transcendent experience. It commanded the attention
of all alike; the intelligentsia, the so-called low brow; the rich and
poor; the thousands or one. He was always sincere, moving and
vibrant, alert to his duty toward the performance of his music. He
always set the vibrations he desired in a room . . .

While he was firm in insisting that absolute adherence to the musical
score be maintained, he was always sympathetic to any suggestion
given by his singers. There was, for instance, the Sportin' Life of the
New York cast (John W. Bubbles) who had experienced great success
on the vaudeville stage and who was not too particular about a musical
score with symphonic accompaniment. The singer much preferred the
'ad lib'; further, this individual would hold a particular note two beats
on Monday night but on Tuesday night he might sustain that same
note through six beats. Consequently, this very fine actor would conceive and reconceive Mr Gershwin's score as often as he sang it.
Frequently, George Gershwin's keen sense of humor would help him
over what might have been a tragic moment between singer and
composer, not to speak of tilts between singer and . . . conductor.

Todd Duncan, 'Memoirs of George Gershwin', *George Gershwin*, Merle
Armitage, ed. (New York, 1938), pp. 63–4

OSCAR LEVANT

His presence on one occasion doubtless saved, for the audience that
subsequently enjoyed it, one of the great performances of *Porgy* – the
'Sporting Life' of Bubbles . . . [whose] negligence about rehearsals
and promptness almost overbalanced his abilities, however; and on one
occasion [conductor Alexander] Smallens' exasperation with the absent
Bubbles caused him to fling down his baton and shout to Mamoulian,
'I'm sick of this waiting. We'll have to throw him out and get somebody else.'

Gershwin bounded from his seat a few rows back in the darkened theater and rushed down the aisle.

'Throw him out?' he said. 'You can't do that. Why, he's – he's the black Toscanini!'

Oscar Levant, *A Smattering of Ignorance* (New York, 1941), pp. 179–80

VERNON DUKE

I went to Boston with George for the tryout. At the orchestra rehearsal he grinned with delight at the well-organized sound that emerged from the pit. I was sitting quietly in a seat in the last row of the orchestra when George startled me by suddenly appearing from the back and grabbing me by the shoulder. 'Hey, Dukie!' he whispered fiercely. 'Just listen to those overtones!' One day he played the ingenious 'crap game' fugue . . . his face beaming. 'Get this – Gershwin writing fugues! What will the boys say now!'

Vernon Duke, *Passport to Paris* (Boston, 1955), p. 312

J. ROSAMOND JOHNSON
(1873–1954)

A graduate of the New England Conservatory of Music, J. Rosamond Johnson was a composer, author, conductor, actor and singer. He portrayed 'Lawyer Frazier' in the original 1935 production of *Porgy and Bess*, as well as in the 1942 revival.

It was in Boston at the close of the first public performance of *Porgy and Bess*. George Gershwin smiled graciously in his own inimitable manner. He had witnessed the child of his brain, had heard the unanimous applause from the audience. As he stood there on the stage of the Colonial Theatre, I was amazed at the modest manner in which he received many warm and hearty congratulations. Finally, when I got a chance to grasp his hand, I whispered to him, 'George, you've done it – you're the Abraham Lincoln of Negro music.'

J. Rosamond Johnson, 'Emancipator of American Idioms', *George Gershwin*, Merle Armitage, ed. (New York, 1938), p. 65

KAY SWIFT

The opening was great. During the intermission we went out into the alley . . . and I remember (vocalist) Libby Holman saying, 'George, it's so great I haven't stopped crying,' and she was sobbing right then. Everybody was. It was so moving. The critics didn't know what hit them – they ate their words later.

Robert Kimball and Alfred Simon, *The Gershwins* (New York, 1973), p. 188

GEORGE GERSHWIN

Since the opening of *Porgy and Bess* I have been asked frequently why it is called a folk opera. The explanation is a simple one. *Porgy and Bess* is a folk tale. Its people would naturally sing folk music. When I first began work on the music I decided against the use of original folk material because I wanted the music to be all of one piece. Therefore I wrote my own spirituals and folksongs. But they are still folk music – and therefore, being in operatic form, *Porgy and Bess* becomes a folk opera.

However, because *Porgy and Bess* deals with Negro life in America it brings to the operatic form elements that have never appeared in opera and I have adapted my method to utilize the drama, the humor, the superstition, the religious fervor, the dancing and the irrepressible high spirits of the race. If, in doing this, I have created a new form, which combines opera with theatre, this new form has come quite naturally out of the material.

It is true that I have written songs for *Porgy and Bess*. I am not ashamed of writing songs at any time so long as they are good songs.

George Gershwin, 'Rhapsody in Catfish Row', *New York Times*, 20 October 1935

VII

The Pundits: Pro and Con

Once *Rhapsody in Blue* made the name of Gershwin he became fair game for cultural Big Thinkers. He vexed them. What made him especially appealing was his apparent double life, straddling the abyss between Tin Pan Alley and Carnegie Hall. Where did he belong? Which would last: the songs or the 'serious' compositions? And what about that awful jazz? (It should be noted that few, if any, critics of Gershwin's time had any idea of what jazz was; it was not until the thirties that writing about true jazz surfaced – and the usually white authorities had little good to say about Gershwin and the self-proclaimed 'King of Jazz', Paul Whiteman.) So Gershwin provided critics and reviewers of all persuasions with substance for speculative essays – newspapers, periodicals, books. While denied the benefit of hindsight, some of these writers seem to have been right about Gershwin and his work; others were surpassingly wrong.

GILBERT SELDES

(1893–1970)

Gilbert Seldes was an early student of the popular arts: comic strips, films, popular song, musical comedy, vaudeville, the circus, etc. In 1924 he published a volume of his views entitled *The 7 Lively Arts* (reissued in 1957, when he commented and expanded on these earlier appraisals). Seldes had been a newspaper correspondent, wrote editorials for *Collier's* magazine and worked for a time for an avant-garde magazine, *The Dial*. He later became a director with Columbia Broadcasting System's television division.

Two composers are possible successors to [Irving] Berlin if he ever chooses to stop. I omit Jerome Kern – a consideration of musical style will indicate why. I am sure of Gershwin and would be more sure of Cole Porter if his astonishing lyrics did not so dazzle me as to make me distrust my estimate of his music. Gershwin is in Berlin's tradition; he has almost all the older man's qualities as a composer (not as a lyric writer; nor has he Berlin's sense of a song on the stage).* That is to say, Gershwin is capable of everything, from 'Swanee' to 'A Stairway to Paradise'. His sentiment is gentler than Berlin's, his 'attack' more delicate. Delicacy, even dreaminess, is a quality he alone brings into jazz music. And his sense of variation in rhythm, of an oddly placed accent, of emphasis and color, is impeccable. He isn't of the stage, yet, so he lacks Berlin's occasional bright hardness; he never has Berlin's smartness; and with a greater musical knowledge he seems possessed of an insatiable interest and curiosity. I feel I can bank on him.

Gilbert Seldes, *The 7 Lively Arts* (New York, 1927), p. 92

Gershwin was not only hailed by the critics, he was positively 'taken up' by the *café society* which was just then coming into being. An intense, enormously self-centred, handsome and utterly likeable person, he might have been spoiled by his quick success. I see no indication in his work that he deflected for a moment from his natural direction. The only phrase in all I wrote of him that he picked out for comment was 'insatiable interest and curiosity'. How did I guess that, he asked me, and I could only answer that he seemed to me to be trying half a dozen styles in order to discover the one exactly right for him. He found it and it carried him into the theatre and eventually into opera.

Gilbert Seldes, *The 7 Lively Arts* (New York, rev. edn, 1957), p. 93

It is ten years since I heard George Gershwin betray any interest in the opinions of critics, so I hope he will not be too much offended at being considered a case. Like most other human beings, Gershwin has been pushed around a bit, but on the whole he hasn't been pushed out of his own direction. He knows what he is doing, even when he is doing too much or doing the wrong thing. A long time ago he wasn't

*This was obviously written before the production of *Lady, be Good!* in 1924.

feeling well and his doctor put him on regimens and Gershwin had a little notebook in which he recorded his diet and other details; he knew exactly what he was doing. I do not suppose he has a notebook with charts for his musical progress, but he is a young man with assurance. If he is going to do an opera this year, you may be sure that this fits into a general plan which may include a movie theme song or a tone poem or a popular melody for next year. If he decides not to compose for six months and amuse himself by painting, he will have in mind the results of his vacation on the next season's output. There is nothing calculating or timid about this; Gershwin will try anything because he is really Kipling's child with his 'satiable curiosity'. At the same time he is too well established to be blown away by any wind of chance. I don't know any popular American composer who is brighter, more generally aware, more likely to give you mental satisfaction than Gershwin, and, the moment this is said, I ought to go on and indicate my doubt whether Gershwin is really a popular composer at all . . .

There is a famous bit of dialogue along Tin Pan Alley: How long will Gershwin's music live? As long as Gershwin is alive to play it! He loves a piano, and it is said that no amount of sarcasm and no show of force will keep him away – and he is right, because he is one of the most entertaining of all pianists . . . His darting mind controls his darting fingers, his playing is as amusing as his melodies are tricky and smart. But he pays for his skill. Popular music used to be written to be sung; then to be danced to; and now it is written to be played . . . And Gershwin's become more and more songs to be played. They are masterly: 'I've [sic] got rhythm' (and could you ask for anything more?), 'Strike up the Band', 'Sam and Delilah', and the best thing in two successive shows, 'Wintergreen for President'. No one has ever sung, no one has ever tried, no one was ever meant to try, to sing 'Wintergreen for President'. But who can forget it?

Not Gershwin, in any case. What he can play on the piano – and he can play anything – he puts down on paper, forgetting that we who listen are not gifted with his mastery of complicated rhythms. So he composes to be heard, not to be sung. He is lucky because we are becoming a nation of listeners, thanks to the radio. But he is losing ground as a pure troubadour. He has stopped singing himself. Privately there is a lot of simplicity in Gershwin. He is young, he is successful, he enjoys his success. Whenever you see him, he is overwhelmed in work, mad about some new dancer or singer who is going to put over something he has composed, rehearsing with a cigar handy, dashing back to his penthouse which was modern (and strikingly and comfortably modern) at the very beginning of the rage for modern, thinking about going to Hollywood, discussing a new lyric with his brother Ira who lives on the same terrace and comes in ready with something intricate in rhyme-schemes to make sure that brother George doesn't fall back on June and Moon. He is tall and dark and looks well in tails and always looks a little self-conscious when he is not working; not uncomfortable in the world of expensive clubs, but aware of them; not overcome by people nearly as famous as himself, but nodding to them; not dazzled but pleased.

That likeable simplicity doesn't come out in his work which gets more complicated and interesting and brittle and unmelodious with every year. It is as if Gershwin were writing for the five thousand people who go to the Lido, know the best club in London, can't count above 21 in New York, and depend on Elsa Maxwell for a good time. Those five thousand – perhaps there are a few more – making up the bulk of the first week's audiences at a new show, can give a musical piece an invisible banner to fly from the theatre's marquee, worth as much as a Pulitzer prize; the wit and intelligence which pleases them can then bring in the fifty thousand more who are needed to pay off the cost of production. But they cannot make a popular composer.

At bottom, I do not believe that Gershwin is a satirist. I can't be sure, but I do not think he has suffered enough or thought enough; he hasn't had time, success coming to him early, frequently and abundantly. I think he has been carried away by the satire of others. There was a middle point when Gershwin wrote a musical burlesque with lyrics by Brian Hooker, of which the masterpiece, words and music, was 'Innocent Ingenue (Baby)'. The show* was not a success and the songs are remembered by perhaps a dozen people, of whom I am the most persistent. Here you had a sweet melody with a touch of mockery on the word 'Baby'; but when you come to 'Of thee I sing, Baby', the satire is everything. It rises to a high level of satisfaction when you dance off with a hey-nonny-nonny and a hotchacha or hear cheers for your own country and s-s-s for the Swiss, the music in these cases being apt and full of bright little ideas. There isn't anyone else

*Our Nell (1922); 'Innocent Ingenue Baby' is credited also to William Daly.

who could let music ripple so freely around the Supreme Court and the Senate and Communists and depressions. A touch of parody here, a shift of emphasis or rhythm making a marching song pompous and ridiculous, a sharp or a flat when you are not expecting either to show that a love song isn't to be taken seriously, and a lightness of touch everywhere, making the whole gay and bright – Gershwin has them in profusion, he is a cascade of little inventions, he gives you a good time.* The reason is that he has a good time himself with his music. When he discovered himself on the road to a new position in America – a composer of jazz who was to be played by symphony orchestras – be began to study orchestration, fascinated by it, by the instruments and their voices. He was young enough not to abandon the effort to learn all the technical business of writing music: harmony and counterpoint and dividing voices. And he didn't let his concert work slide, either; from a trip abroad he brought back *An American in Paris* and he wrote a concerto for orchestra and himself ('for orchestra with piano' on the programs, of course, and I believe others have played it, but probably not so well.)† In the old days when Otto Kahn was being liberally misquoted as wanting a 'jazz opera' for the Metropolitan, Gershwin was coming over the horizon as the man who might make what Kahn really wanted, a grand opera using the rhythms of American popular music. My own guess is that Gershwin will do better with an American ballet . . . I'd rather see him do that than do an operatic version of *Porgy* which I never succumbed to in the first place. I'd rather see him doing a ballet than have him write songs which might have been written by Cole Porter (only Gershwin's are essentially innocent). Give a good ballet master the *Stairway to Paradise* (reworked by the author, because it is over ten years old now and Gershwin has learned a lot) and you'd have the foundation of a ballet right there. Or, his own Variations on 'I've [sic] got rhythm'. Or anything he has written in five years.

Gilbert Seldes, 'The Gershwin Case', *Esquire*, October 1934, p. 130

---

*Seldes is referring to the political operettas, *Strike up the Band, Of Thee I Sing* and *Let 'em Eat Cake*.
†The *Second Rhapsody for Orchestra with Piano*

PAUL ROSENFELD
(1890–1946)

Paul Rosenfeld was best known as a perceptive music critic, although he also wrote about art and artists, photography and literature. His writings appeared in such literary–political publications as *The Dial*, *The New Republic* and *Seven Arts*. One of his most interesting books is *An Hour with American Music* in which he presented essays on contemporary American composers, including Carlos Chávez and Edgar Varèse. The volume begins with an essay on jazz that opens with the words, 'American music is not jazz. Jazz is not music,' and proceeds to reveal that like so many of his colleagues, he had no idea of what jazz was. Nor was he an admirer of Gershwin.

Gershwin's *Rhapsody in Blue*, Piano Concerto and *An American in Paris* have found a good deal of popular favor; and Gershwin himself is assuredly a gifted composer of the lower, unpretentious order; yet there is some question whether his vision permits him an association with the artists. He seems to have little feeling for reality. His compositions drowse one in a pink world of received ideas and sentiments; The *Rhapsody in Blue* is circus-music, preeminent in the sphere of tinsel and fustian. In daylight, nonetheless, it stands vaporous with its second-hand ideas and ecstasies; its old-fashioned Lisztian ornament and brutal, calculated effects, not so much music, as jazz dolled up. Gershwin's concerto has an equal merit. The opening of the second movement, the Blues section, is charming and atmospheric; but the work is utterly bare of the impulsion toward a style which every living thing exhibits; and, like the *Rhapsody*, scarcely transcends the level of things made to please an undiscriminating public. *An American in Paris* is poorer in themes than either of its predecessors; and when, after losing its way, the music turns into the lively somewhat meaningless sort of flourish usually supplied the finales of musical comedy first-acts, we seem to hear Gershwin's instrument, like Balaam's ass, reproving the false prophet;* directing him to the sphere congenial to his gift.

Paul Rosenfeld, *An Hour with American Music* (Philadelphia, 1929), pp. 138–9

George Gershwin's rhapsodies and other pieces in the symphonic form have inspired certain critics to classify him as a good 'vulgar' composer . . . 'Notre Chabrier à nous', one critic, adapting d'Indy's epithet for Debussy, affectionately called him. This judgement is extremely uncritical, exhibiting a defective vision of good 'vulgar' music and of Gershwin's ambitious product and the difference between them. That many of the expressions found in our Broadway paladin's two rhapsodies and his Piano Concerto, his *An American in Paris* and his *Cuban Overture*, formerly the *Rumba*, are popular and American, is certain. Not the earliest symphonic works merging or attempting to merge the expressions of Broadway with traditional and personal expressions – for Satie's *Parade* and a number of pieces of the Parisian Six represented this tendency before the *Rhapsody in Blue* – Gershwin's absolute and programmatic compositions are distinguished by their frequent, sometimes vivacious and adroit, at other times coarse and brutal, exploitations of the jazz idioms, rhythms, and colors. That the result is representative of a certain kind of American is also certain; their immense popular success is one proof of it. Yet to qualify as a vulgar composer and rank with Chabrier, Albéniz, Glinka, and even with Milhaud and Auric at their best, a musician has to 'compose' his material, to sustain and evolve and organize it to a degree sufficient to bring its essence, their relationships, their ideas, to expression. And that Gershwin has accomplished to no satisfactory degree, at least not in any of the larger forms he has up to the present time given the public.

Take any one of his amibitious products. It is only very superficially a whole, actually a heap of extremely heterogeneous minor forms and expressions. Individually these minor forms and expressions, themes, melodies, rhythms, harmonies, figures, ornaments, are frequently piquant and striking, and richly dissonant, and brilliantly colored.

*Balaam (Numbers 22–3), ordered by Balak, King of the Moabites, to curse the Israelites, blesses them instead, after being rebuked by his faithful donkey (with a little help from the Angel of the Lord).

But they are extremely disparate, first of all in point of freshness. Some are the raciest of rhythmic and coloristic neologisms, effective exploitations of various elements of the jazz idiom or original material. Others are very worn and banal. Again, they remain equally disparate in point of style, some of them being popularly American in essence or gaily, brightly Yiddish, and others impressionistic, or vaguely grand-operatic, or reminiscent of the melodramatic emphasis and *fioritura* of Liszt, or Chopinesque. And they also remain disparate in point of quality, since a number of them have sharpness, jauntiness, dash, indicating a perhaps shallow but distinct vitality, while others are weak, soft, cheap, representing a vitality duller and lower than that at which interest commences – so soft and cheap indeed that in comparison with them the best of Gershwin's ideas, maugre the fact that very few of them have the delicacy and power of first-rate stuff and that his treatment of jazz is by no means highly sensitive, appear almost the expression of another man . . .

Take the juiciest and most entertaining of Gershwin's concert works, the F major Piano Concerto. It commences with a number of disconnected flourishes. At length the composer comes to grips with his material: the first original theme enters, syncopated, impassioned, on the piano. It is repeated by the saxophone in a low register, and by the piano, and after short divertissements, twice by the *tutti*, the last time with decided dash. A certain tension has been created, impelling one to look forward to some sort of contrast and development. What now follows, however, is an irrelevant theme, very popular, and in a Charleston measure. For a period the music flows. Sometimes lyrical, sometimes merely rhetorical, the page is one of Gershwin's most sustained and charmingly orchestrated expressions. But it, too, stops short of completion. And after a brief polyphonic passage the first theme is restated with inflations recalling some of the grandiose effects of the Capital Theatre . . .

The second movement begins with an interesting, muted treatment of a blues theme; but after the melody has been stated and we have been led to look forward to some inevitable development, the composer introduces some more material which one would call similar to the original blues theme were it not so very much inferior to that original theme in quality. All tension has disappeared. The impulse of the beginning is entirely let down. The weak material grows pathetic amid strains of Liebestod. And the movement is concluded with a nostalgic little coda made from the 'blues' theme .

Hope that the composer is going to get somewhere has entirely dwindled, and though the last movement begins vigorously with a good scherzando theme for the xylophone, one is not surprised to find the movement largely a recapitulation of old material, leading up to a restatement of the original theme more grandiosely inflated even than any of the preceding ones and concluding inconsequentially with further flourishes. While the succeeding composition, the tripartite *An American in Paris*, starts somewhat more energetically, it too, has no real movement . . . and with the exception of the amusing passage imitative of French motor horns, the material itself is less attractive than that of the ritzy concerto. Thus, deficiently expressive of essences and ideas, even the lighter, saltier, more comic ones that are the vulgar American composer's objects, these strings of melodies and rhythms put one in touch with little that is real. Momentarily we feel the forces of ambition and desire; imperious, unmitigated appetites, yearnings for tenderness, intoxications flowing from the stimulation of novel, luxurious surroundings, Parisian, Cuban, Floridian, from the joy of feeling oneself an American – Americanism apparently conceived as a naïve, smart, inept, good-natured form of being, happily and humorously shared by other good fellows like oneself – and from a gaminlike eroticism . . . It is impossible to hear Gershwin's symphonic music without being from time to time moved by its grandiloquences to conceive – with the aspect of things having some immensely flattering, glorifying bearing upon ourselves – of towers of fine gold rising amid Florida palms, splendiferous hotel foyers crowded with important people and gorgeous women *décolletées jusqu'à là*, and immediately contingent upon paradise; or rosy banks of nymphs amorously swooning amid bells of rose-pink tulle. A tawny oriental city acknowledges us as its conquerer in the sundown, and the superb naked woman who stands above the city gate, starred with the diamond in her tresses, descends and advances toward us with exalted words and gestures, hailing our peerlessness while we ourselves recognize in her one we have always sought and loved. Are these atrocious dreams our own? Possibly, but they have grown articulate through this music.

. . . most American art is advertising, glorifying the material objects and fanning up the appetite directed upon them; and this category of aesthetic products is dangerously close to that of George Gershwin. Indeed, we are tempted to call Gershwin the laureate of musical advertisers, perhaps the most genial of them all, but the head of their company; the musician of the materialistic age that saw the bloom of the worst business and best advertising America has ever endured, the jazz age . . .

Of course it is possible that the idea of the musicians who called him our vulgar composer was entirely prophetic and that Gershwin is not yet but will be the music interpreter of what the ordinary American feels in his genuine living moments. The event is certainly not without the bounds of possibility. Gershwin is still a relatively young man. There is no question of his talent. The musical language is natively his own: one can see he was not introduced to it yesterday, that he knows it and feels and likes it, and has a decided knack with it. He has spontaneity, an ear for complex rhythms, a feeling for luscious, wistful, dissonantly harmonized melodies. Above all, he has a distinctive warmth; and if the main honors for the symphonic exploitation and idealization of jazz have gone to Milhaud for *La Création du Monde*, to Honegger for his Piano Concertino, and to Copland for his Piano Concerto, rather more than to himself, he at least stands almost gigantically among the other sons of Tin Pan Alley, Bennett, Levant, Grofé, who have grappled with more or less symphonic forms. At least he has a veritable urgency and a spirit of endeavor that commands sympathy. Only, we remain unconvinced that he has sufficient of the feeling of the artist. The artist's remoteness from material objects, his suspended, selfless, aesthetic touch of them, his tension and experience of order, and his impulse to organize his material in conformity with that experience – we have not as yet caught more than a fleeting glance of them in Gershwin's products. We remain obliged to him mostly for *Funny Face* and his other smart musical shows. His talent burgeons in them.

Paul Rosenfeld, 'No Chabrier', *New Republic*, 4 January 1933, pp. 217–18

CONSTANT LAMBERT

(1905–51)

Composer, conductor and author, who studied with Ralph
Vaughan Williams, Constant Lambert wrote his first ballet
for Diaghilev at the age of twenty-one. He explored jazz
in such works as *Elegiac Blues* (1927) and *The Rio Grande*
(1929): charming, delightful and fascinating but hardly
jazz. His book *Music Ho! – A Study of Music in Decline*
is a classic of provocative opinion.

The first-fruits of symphonic jazz have been a little disappointing, it
is true, particularly in the land where they have been most common
– the United States of America. The Americans seem to live too near
Tin Pan Alley to get the beauties of this street in proper perspective;
their pictures of it are either too realistic or too romantic. They
suffer from the immense disadvantage of being on the spot – are not
Rousseau's paintings of tropical landscapes more impressive than those
of Gauguin? The difficulty of making a satisfactory synthesis of jazz
is due to the fact that it is not, properly speaking, raw material
but half-finished material in which European sophistication has been
imposed over coloured crudity. There is always the danger that the
highbrow composer may take away the number he first thought of and
leave only the sophisticated trappings behind. This is indeed what has
happened in that singularly inept albeit popular piece, Gershwin's
Rhapsody in Blue. The composer, trying to write a Lisztian concerto
in jazz style, has used only the non-barbaric elements in dance music,
the result being neither good jazz nor good Liszt, and in no sense of
the word a good concerto. Although other American composers, and
even Gershwin himself, have produced works of greater calibre in
this style, the shadow of the *Rhapsody in Blue* hangs over most of them
and they remain the hybrid child of a hybrid. A rather knowing and
unpleasant child too, ashamed of its parents and boasting of its French
lessons.

Constant Lambert, *Music Ho!* (London, 1934) pp. 194–5

RALPH VAUGHAN WILLIAMS
(1872–1958)

One of Britain's greatest humanist-musicians, Ralph
Vaughan Williams composed many works, including symphonies, magnificent choral settings, songs, arrangements
of folksongs, sacred and film music. He was also a man
of wisdom and perception, as demonstrated in his letters,
speeches and writings, which include three brief, but idea-
packed books.

We must not make the mistake of thinking lightly of the very characteristic art of Gershwin or, to go further back, the beautiful melodies
of Stephen Foster. Great things grow out of small beginnings. The
American composers who wrote symphonic poems for which they were
not emotionally ready, are forgotten, while the work of those who
attempted less and achieved more has become the foundation on which
a great art can rise.

Ralph Vaughan Williams, *The Making of Music* (New York, 1955)

VIRGIL THOMSON
(1896–1989)

Composer, critic and author, Virgil Thomson is probably
best known for his operatic collaborations with Gertrude
Stein, (especially *Four Saints in Three Acts*). He was a
witty, often devastating writer on music, and served as
music critic of the *New York Herald-Tribune* during the
1940s and 1950s. He composed outstanding scores for
films, including *The Plough That Broke the Plains*, *The
River* and *Louisiana Story*. Thomson belonged to the estab-
lishment of American contemporary music, represented by
the League of Composers, which published a quarterly,
Modern Music.

Gershwin, Cole Porter, and Kern are America's Big Three in the light
musical theatre. Their qualities are evident and untroubling. Mr

Gershwin has, however, for some time been leading a double musical life. This is the story of his adventures among the high-brows.

His efforts in the symphonic field cover a period of about twelve years and include, so fas as I am acquainted with them

A Rhapsody in Blue, for piano and orchestra
Harlem Night, a ballet*
Two Concertos, for piano and orchestra†
The [sic] *American in Paris*, a symphonic poem

to which can be added an opera on a tragi-comic subject, *Porgy and Bess*.

The *Rhapsody in Blue*, written about 1924 or 1925, was the first of these and is the most successful from every point of view. It is the most successful orchestral piece ever launched by any American composer. It is by now standard orchestral repertory all over the world, just like Rimsky's *Sheherazade* and Ravel's *Boléro*.

It is a thoroughly professional job executed by a man who knew how to put over a direct musical idea and who had a direct musical idea to put over . . .

Talent, in fact, is rather easier to admire when the intentions of a composer are more noble than his execution is competent . . .

The *Rhapsody in Blue* remains a quite satisfactory piece. Rhapsodies, however, are not very difficult formula, if one can think up enough tunes. The efforts at a more sustained symphonic development which the later pieces represent, appear now to be just as tenuous as they always sounded. One can see through *Porgy* that Gershwin has not and never did have any power of sustained musical development . . . In Gershwin's music the predominance of charm in presentation over expressive substance makes the result always a sort of *vers de société*, or *musique de salon*; and his lack of understanding of all the major problems of form, of continuity, and of serious or direct musical expression is not surprising in view of the impurity of his musical sources and his frank acceptance of same.

Such frankness is admirable. At twenty-five it was also charming. *Gaminerie* of any kind at thirty-five is more difficult to stomach. So that quite often *Porgy and Bess*, instead of being pretty, is a little

*Thomson may be referring to *Blue Monday*, a one-act opera with dancing.
†Gershwin composed only one concerto and two rhapsodies, which may have confused Thomson.

hoydenish, like a sort of *musique de la pas très bonne société*. Leaving aside the slips even and counting him at his best, that best which is equally well exemplified by *Lady, be Good!* or 'I've [sic] got rhythm', or the opening of the *Rhapsody in Blue*, he is still not a very serious composer.

. . . *Porgy* is none the less an interesting example of what can be done by talent in spite of a bad set-up. With a libretto that should never have been accepted on a subject that should never have been chosen, a man who should never have attempted it has written a work that is of some power and importance.

. . . Gershwin does not even know what an opera is; and yet *Porgy and Bess* is an opera and it has power and vigor. Hence it is a more important event in America's artistic life than anything American the Met has ever done . . .

There are many things about it that are not to my personal taste. I don't like fake folk-lore, nor fidgety accompaniments nor bitter-sweet harmony, nor six part choruses, nor plum-pudding orchestration. I do, however, like being able to listen to a work for three hours and to be fascinated at every moment. I also like its lack of respectability, the way it can be popular and vulgar and go its way as a professional piece does without bothering much about the taste-boys. I like to think of Gershwin as having presented his astonished and somewhat perturbed public with a real live baby, all warm and dripping and friendly.

Virgil Thomson, 'George Gershwin', *Modern Music*, November–December 1935, pp. 13–19

FREDERICK JACOBI

(1891–1952)

A composer, teacher and conductor, Frederick Jacobi's compositions include works for orchestra, voice and chamber groups. He is best remembered as a teacher at the Juilliard School of Music, New York (1936–50); his students include Alexei Haiff, Robert Starer and Robert Ward. He was a member of the Executive Board of the League of Composers.

Like his illustrious predecessors, Jacques Offenbach and Sir Arthur Sullivan, Gershwin wanted to burn the candle at both ends: to be both Sinner and Saint, a sort of Madonna of the Sleeping Cars. And, what is still more difficult . . . he wanted to be both at the same time. The effort is commendable but it rarely works! Different moods, different styles and different techniques; and the man who is capable of the one can rarely also master the other.

. . . He wanted to talk both to the Winter Garden and Carnegie Hall – 'Swanee' for the one and for the other the Concerto in F: different pieces, it is true, with different textures and different outward forms. But the message, jazzy and glowing, was to remain about the same . . .

For, though a master within his own small forms, Gershwin was completely beyond his depth in a phrase more than sixteen or thirty-two bars long, in one not regularly constructed on the *last* on which all such phrases are constructed. If Rachmaninoff had only come to his help in bringing 'around the curve' the illustrious Second Theme in the *Rhapsody in Blue*! If he had only been able to extricate himself from the meshes of his own creation in the over-sweet and ill-formed 'Bess, you is my woman now!' These are but fundamentals of phrase structure. For the longer intellectual effort required to sustain a symphonic movement Gershwin was wholly inadequate; nor is there any indication that he realized his shortcomings as an architect. And with his failing craftmanship so also vanished his sense of style. How otherwise explain the laborious and old-fashioned recitatives in *Porgy and Bess* and the indiscriminate and ill-fused mixture which constitutes so large a part of the idiom of that work? Gershwin who, at his best, not only has his own individual style but who also possesses that supreme thing called: style! The effectiveness of those parts of *Porgy and Bess* which are effective is for the most part based on well-known theatrical and musical clichés . . . 'It ain't necessarily so!' How that small piece, lean and wiry stands out in its place, like a black diamond in the fog! Here Gershwin is himself again with no lapses into the vulgar, no departures from his usual good taste. How strange that Gershwin should, in his larger and more pretentious works, lack precisely those qualities which are otherwise so much his own: style, shape and that indefinable thing called authenticity, that sense of something freshly felt rather than of something heavily constructed!

. . . It is not in his 'larger' works that George will live. It is in the great number of his songs, almost every one of which is a gem in its own way . . . Who can forget the insinuating melodic line of 'You don't know the half of it, Dearie, Blues'? The perfection of harmony and form which is in 'The man I love'? The subtle irony of the masterpiece: 'Mine' from *Let 'em Eat Cake*? The bawdy and really marvelous little climax in 'Sam and Delilah'? The dry, pulsating surge of 'Fascinating Rhythm', 'Clap yo' hands' and 'High Hat' – off-center and fantastically poised, as a moment in a dance by Fred Astaire? *Lisa!* [sic] *Lady, be Good! Who Cares!* Who of us has not felt their glow and exhilarating sense of careless, high enjoyment with which they are suffused?

. . . George was undoubtedly very fortunate in having in his brother, Ira, a marvelous collaborator. The most perfect wedding of their talents was, perhaps, in *Of Thee I Sing* which, as a whole, is unique in the annals of the Gershwins and of the American stage. One need not underestimate the importance of Ira in bringing to fruition the talents of George. But the music of George is something in itself and in his tragic and premature passing America has lost one of its brightest stars . . . He belongs in the company of those blissful demi-gods, Sullivan, Offenbach and Johann Strauss, men who have evoked immediate response in the hearts of their contemporaries, men who have been the articulate expression of their age and who have, to an extent granted to few, molded their age and become a symbol of what it was. Their vein has been rich and complete.

And so it has been with George.

Frederick Jacobi, 'The Future of Gershwin', *Modern Music*, November–December 1937, pp. 3–7

OLIN DOWNES

On the day of Gershwin's death, *New York Times* critic Olin Downes wrote an essay about the composer published in conjunction with Gershwin's obituary. Like Jacobi, he attempted to fit Gershwin into a neat category. The headline of the piece read: 'Gershwin Caused New Jazz Values'; one of the subheads: 'Did Not Imitate Masters'.

George Gershwin has a unique position in American music, one due in part to his wholly exceptional gifts and in part to a special set of circumstances which raised him in less than five years from the rank of a song plugger in Tin Pan Alley to that of a composer whose works invaded symphony concert programs and operatic auditoriums and made him internationally famous. In some respects, and partly by virtue of the immense amount of publicity he received, his value may have been exaggerated . . .

He never passed a certain point as a 'serious composer'. It was not in him to do what Dvořák did for Bohemian music, or even for American music in the 'New World' Symphony, or what Grieg did for Norway in his art. Gershwin had too limited a technic for that, and the greater forms, because of his beginnings, were never really natural to him.

But in his most characteristic scores he struck out a vein of his own, sufficiently fresh, new, natural and racy to command wide attention and to refresh enormously the ears in a period which offers little that is new and original in musical creation. Some would see in his rise a manifestation of a certain phase of democracy and American opportunity. His emergence from the stage of a highly promising purveyor of popular entertainment to the higher realms of art began when one day the singer Eva Gauthier walked into Harms Music Shop and asked the young Gershwin if he would play her accompaniment while she sang some American popular songs by him in Boston and New York, offering him for this special service something more than his accustomed $2 an hour.*

At first the young man at the piano did not understand the proposition, but he finally accepted, and soon was famous. The songs, by their swing, their wit, their original rhythmic and harmonic settings of the texts, made an absolutely novel sensation when they fell on ears habituated to, but also perhaps fatigued by, over-intellectualized products of certain cerebral modern European composers. It may be added that no small part of the effect was furnished by Gershwin's playing.

Those who have not heard him accompany his songs do not suspect

*By 1923, the year of Gauthier's recital, Gershwin had been on the staff of the T. B. Harms Co. (not Music Shop) as a staff composer at a salary of more than $2 an hour, for several years.

their full flavor. These accompaniments have never been fully written down. They cannot be, Gershwin had a tone, a touch and a rhythm not easily described. The accompaniments were themselves tone-pictures, however trivial or merely topical the character of the song might be. And they possessed one of the most distinctive characteristics of our American jazz – the element of improvisation. They also constituted an extraordinary commentary on Ira Gershwin's texts. The texts have not received their proper praise. They were made for George's special musical gift as George had precisely the style to set off the verses of Ira. This was the beginning of Gershwin's reputation . . .

Sometimes it seems that Gershwin was given too great a responsibility by musicians and critics so eager to see a real school of American composition developed that they encouraged him to more serious paths than those he was born to follow. But certainly he pointed the way, even though the first act of *Of Thee I Sing* and passages from his best light operas will rank much higher than any part of his attempted 'folk opera', (*Porgy*); and though some of his topical or risqué little songs carry a lilt of melody and a wealth of innuendo that outshine more serious attempts in real life and individuality.

A new step was taken by Gershwin for American music, a step that more pretentious composers were unable to execute. The sum of his achievement will make him live long in the record of American music.

Olin Downes, *New York Times*, 12 July 1937, p. 20

> The jazz historians, critics and collectors of 'hot' records flourished after Gershwin's death; few forgave him for not knowing what the True Jazz was, nor for his association with the false 'King', Paul Whiteman. The consensus is pretty well summed up in the following selections. What is ignored is the fascination Gershwin's songs had for the true jazzmen, who often based their performances on the chord structures, the harmonies and rhythms of these little pieces. They were the basis for beautiful improvisations by eminent jazz musicians ranging from Pee Wee Russell, through Art Tatum, Coleman Hawkins and Charlie Parker.

RALPH DE TOLENDANO

(b. 1916)

As a young jazz enthusiast, Ralph de Tolendano was a co-founder and editor of the short-lived scholarly periodical *Jazz Information* in the late 1930s. After serving in the Second World War, he was a some-time editor and businessman.

The 'jazz as art' movement has been going on ever since Paul Whiteman's Aeolian Hall concert when George Gershwin gave up writing good songs for bad concert pieces. From the first it fed on the plaudits of jazz illiterates among the musical great – Stokowski, Damrosch, and Co, – then the equally senseless attacks of the academicians whose idea of the real product was Henry Busse's sour rendition of *Hot Lips*. When a studious commentator discovered that there was a schematic relationship between the so-called Chicago style and the polyphony of Bach, the faddists were off in a blizzard of misapprehension . . .

The faddists were desperately in need of something which could give this new esthetic vapors, and the general public panted along with them. They were ready for that miscegenetic marriage of jazz to Whiteman which resulted in the still-birth of 'symphonic' jazz in the form of the *Rhapsody in Blue* and its many successors. The literature of the period is full of enthusiastic talk on the theory of symphonic jazz, most of which boils down to several world-shaking facts: that Shostakovich used Youmans' 'Tea For Two' as a theme; that Stravinsky employed certain elements of ragtime in some of his work; that Brahms was attracted to the rhythmic effects of 1890 jazz and even contemplated using them in a composition. With this encouragement added to the tinkle of the cash register, hacks who thought of jazz as nothing more than discord and the use of flatted thirds and sevenths to create a 'blue' effect, began to turn out jazz symphonies, rhapsodies, tone poems, and other allied types of musical hash by the yard – while critics who would have turned up their noses at such lack of simple competence in academic forms raved over a 'renascence'.

Ralph de Tolendano, 'Directions of Jazz', *Frontiers of Jazz* (New York, 1947), pp. 66–7

RUDI BLESH

(1899–1985)

After completion of his studies at the University of California Rudi Blesh became a commercial artist, industrial designer and lecturer on design at the San Francisco Museum of Art. An interest in classic jazz led to another career: lecturing on jazz and jazz artists. He formed a recording company specializing in recording jazz performances and wrote two books on the subject, *Shining Trumpets* and, with Harriet Janis, *They All Played Ragtime*.

. . . while Paul Whiteman and George Gershwin and a host of others outside jazz began to 'improve' it and try to make of it symphony, concerto, and opera (all the things it was not, and which, if it needed ever to become, it needed to become by its own means), men like Louis Armstrong were at work within the utmost core of jazz. . . . Jazz is not a mere 'jazzy' rendering, say, of a Beethoven minuet. For this is only a manner of playing with no real transformation of the material. Even less jazz, is the Gershwin *Rhapsody in Blue* that treats quasi harmonies and certain jazz instrumental traits in a symphonic manner. And the music of Whiteman and the various 'jazz symphonists' misses the mark by employing jazz material in a completely non-jazz manner . . . To come to the present, Gershwin's *Porgy and Bess* is not Negro opera despite a Negro cast, a liberal use of artificial coloration, and the inclusion of some street cries. It is *Negroesque*, and the earlier travesty of minstrelsy is continued in a form more subtle and therefore more invidious. This work and more recent ones . . . betray a more deplorable tendency than mere superficiality and lack of understanding. By enlisting actual Negroes for the public performance of these Tin Pan Alley potpourri, a new stereotype – this time a cultural one – is being fitted to the Negro in which he is set forth as an able entertainer singing a music that the white public finds to be just like *its own*. In these works, as in virtually all of the movie output which pretends to present Negro music, the public never hears fine, real Negro music; its delight with it is like that of the Saratoga audience which saw real Negro minstrels with cork-blackened faces.

Rudi Blesh, *Shining Trumpets* (New York, 1953), pp. 13, 195, 205

Around the mid-fifties the conventional attitude toward Gershwin changed. Historians, musicologists – even critics of another generation, free of the usual prejudices – viewed Gershwin from new perspectives. Tin Pan Alley was long-gone, the American musical theatre acquired new respectability, and the line between the musical and opera all but disappeared. It was learned eventually that Gershwin had had a better musical training than most thought. His works, unfortunately edited (even re-orchestrated) by others were returned to their original state, as Gershwin conceived them. This was especially notably demonstrated with *Porgy and Bess*. In its restored original form it became to many, but not of course all, America's 'greatest opera'. That this was essentially true was evident in the perceptive writings of two eminent musicologist–historians, one British, the other American in two of the finest studies of American music extant.

WILFRED MELLERS
(b. 1914)

Musicologist, teacher, author and composer, Wilfred Mellers was a graduate of Cambridge University, where he studied with Egon Wellesz. He taught music in Britain as well as in the US, and has composed in many forms, including opera, orchestral and vocal works. Among his writings are *Music and Society* (1946), *The Sonata Principle* (1957), *Music in a New Found Land* (1965), *Caliban Reborn* (1967), *Twilight of the Gods: The Music of the Beatles* (1973), etc.

George Gershwin was not, like Porgy, a Negro, nor, in the material benefits of life, was he in any way deprived. He was, however, a poor boy who made good: an American Jew who knew all about spiritual isolation and, in Tin Pan Alley, had opportunity enough to learn about corruption. He was not, like Porgy, a physical cripple. He was, however, an emotional cripple, being victimized, like so many of his generation, by nervous maladjustments and the usual escapes from them. So, in his opera, he sang with honesty and with unexpected strength of the spiritual malaise that is inherent in the twentieth-century pop song itself. His instinct for the nostalgia at the heart of the common man's experience rivals that of Stephen Foster: what makes him so much richer a composer is that his art intuitively recognizes the nostalgia as such. His opera is about the impact of the world of commerce on those who once led, would like to have led, may still lead the 'good life', based on a close relationship between man and nature.

Wilfred Mellers, *Music in a New Found Land* (New York, 1965), pp. 392–3

GILBERT CHASE
(b. 1906)

Musicologist, pianist and author, Gilbert Chase graduated from Columbia University. He is an authority on the music of Latin America and was consultant to the American State Department as well as the American Library of Congress. His published works include *The Music of Spain* (1941), *A Guide to the Music of Latin America* (1962) and *America's Music* (1955, rev. 1966).

Gershwin's place in American music is secure. His popular songs will last as long as any music of this type, and his work in the larger forms of art music mark the triumph of the popular spirit in the art music of the United States. Gershwin was a composer of the people and for the people, and his music will be kept alive by the people.

Gilbert Chase, *America's Music* (New York, 1955), p. 493

VIII
Gershwin and Art

George Gershwin's first experience as an aspiring artist had an unhappy ending. Influenced by the cartoons and sketches of his older brother Ira, he made a drawing which he proudly showed to one of his teachers at P.S. 20 on the Lower East Side. She laughed at his attempt. Humiliated before his classmates, he abandoned art for music.

But he would come back to it with a vengeance. Some time in 1927, again under Ira's influence as well as that of his cousin, Henry Botkin ('my cousin, Botkin, the artist'), he took up his pen and pencils once more. During a summer stay at Chumleigh Farm, near Ossining, when not working on the songs for an anti-war musical *Strike up the Band* he and Ira made several drawings. It was Ira who further stimulated his brother by presenting him with a set of watercolour paints. Soon George appeared to spend as much time at the easel as at the keyboard.

There was a period, when George and Ira were writing songs for a Florenz Ziegfeld musical, that the great showman would unexpectedly pop in on the brothers Gershwin to protect his investment; more than once did he surprise them daubing canvases and not creating words and music. (Years later, when a friend asked Ira Gershwin why he had given up painting – for he was a gifted artist – he replied simply, 'It became too interesting.')

George Gershwin pursued art as he did music, with intense vitality; in his mind he closely associated the two. The collector Chester Dale recalled a time when Gershwin, on hearing that Dale had some fascinating paintings, invited himself over. He was particularly impressed with one of Dale's Cézannes. At one point Dale said to Gershwin, 'Music and pictures – aren't they more or less the same?' The composer agreed, then began a monologue on Cézanne that surprised Dale, who thereupon suggested that Gershwin 'play me a Cézanne'. Gershwin went to the

piano and, as Dale put it, 'I haven't got any more idea
than the man in the moon what he played, but emotionally
there was Cézanne to both of us.'

In a brief six years, George Gershwin accumulated one
of the finest collections of contemporary art in the country.
His own efforts made him curious about the works of
others and gallery visits inspired him to collect paintings
by artists he admired. In 1931, when Botkin went to Paris
to paint, he served as Gershwin's guide in collecting. If
he saw something he thought his cousin would like, he
sent a snapshot and description, then Gershwin would
decide if he wanted the work. When he received his first
shipment in June 1931, he wrote enthusiastically to Botkin
(note, the artists he mentions were not so well known as
they are now): 'The Rouault is a gorgeous painting . . .
[it] gives me great pleasure . . . and I hope you will find
some more of his work to send to me.

'The suburbs in Utrillo is painted with a much more
vigorous brush than some of the ones I have seen in
America. It is a very luminous picture. It seems to throw
out its own light. I am crazy about it . . .

'The Derain is a masterpiece of simple color and the
Pascin, while the least exciting of the five, has a strange
quality that seems to grow on me.' (The fifth painting was
a Modigliani, also a favorite.)

Gershwin's collection of more than a hundred works of
art included the now-famous Noguchi bust of himself,
African sculpture, Picasso's 'The Absinthe Drinker' and
works by such Americans as Benton, Bellows, Max Weber
and John Carroll.

Though he prized these pictures and admired their
creators, it is significant that his own original work was
not influenced by them; as in music, he went his own way.
In the eight short years he was active as a painter, sketcher
and watercolourist, he exhibited a growth in draftsmanship
and control of colour. As in his music, there is no selfcon-
sciousness in his paintings and drawings. He gets to the
point, from the complex 'Self Portrait in an Opera Hat'
(1932) to the picturesque and delicately tinted, 'My
Studio, Folly Beach,' (1934). What is fascinating is
that Gershwin excelled at portraiture, certainly the most

challenging subject matter. His own self-portraits are extraordinary and there are fine oils of his grandfather and mother. 'Arnold Schoenberg' and 'Jerome Kern', both done in California in 1937, were his final portraits.

HENRY BOTKIN
(1896–1983)

A noted artist, Henry Botkin was also Gershwin's cousin. He studied at the Massachusetts School of Art, Boston, and at the age of eighteen settled in New York, where he began professionally as an illustrator. In his late twenties he went to Paris where he concentrated on painting, and was introduced to (and deeply influenced by) abstract art. During his early New York decade he spent a good deal of time with his cousins, visiting theatres and museums. While in France he served as George Gershwin's alter-ego in the collection of contemporary art.

A number of years ago George Gershwin experienced his first thrill from a contemporary painting and promptly purchased it with great enthusiasm. At that time he never considered himself a great collector or a champion of modern painting. He bought the canvas because he liked it and wanted it about. It was this irresistible impulse that led to further purchases and the beginning of a most significant collection. Our frequent visits to the galleries and studios of various artists here and abroad displayed George's intense feeling and joy in pictures and painting. The spirit of his music and its relation to art became more and more evident. He realized that his rhythms and their rhythms had many common factors.

His collection has evolved logically and always displays a singleness of purpose and inspiration. He never pretended to possess a scholarly group of paintings, there were no 'old' pictures and he never posed as an art historian or expert. He has striven for examples that seemed to be the most vital and the most stimulating. The careful subtle patterning, the rich color, together with the somber power and fine sentiment found in the various canvases have produced a deep, spontaneous artistic excitement for the collector. During our many years of close relationship, I have noted how the special quality of his extraordinary music has given proof of the similarity of imaginative tendencies and strong spiritual kinship to these many striking achievements in paint. His painting and collecting have resulted in the assimilation of aesthetic nourishment for his musical genius. He was always interested in the various movements of art, but never allowed himself to follow the dictates of fashion. His pictures were not considered as ornaments or decorations for his walls and he was not affected by any intellectual snobbishness.

Art to George seemed ever aglow with passionate life and proved his love for the world of today. Whether he was composing, searching for new masterpieces, painting or joining in a festive evening, he brought to the occasion all the vigor and vital force that was in him. In his adventures in art, if at times he seemed impulsive and spontaneous, he was also simple and highly intelligent. Thus it was that nine years sufficed to bring together one of the most significant collections of modern art in America as well as a group of his own paintings. The collection consists of over a hundred examples of paintings and sculpture, drawings, prints, etc., and though it has no pretense to completeness, it contains some of the greatest examples of contemporary painting that can be found in this country.

George never collected a list of names and it was only the quality of the individual canvases that counted. Some of the most interesting works are the products of the unknown younger painters and not of the men whose names are so familiar to us. They have a definite place in his collection and George championed and assisted them at all times.

Besides paintings in oil by the masters, he had gathered a most varied group of important examples of Negro sculpture, together with drawings, rare watercolors and lithographs. He never confined himself to the paintings of any one group or country, but was always interested in the various movements and schools of art. He possessed some of the most important examples of contemporary art by the dominating personalities in the American art world. Though he was not always sympathetic to abstract art, he studied and collected Kandinsky, Leger, Masson and others. He was extremely interested in Picasso, Utrillo, De Segonzac, Derain and Rousseau. He also possessed some of the outstanding examples of the American school, as, Eilshemius, Bellows, Sterne, Weber and Benton. In recent years his collection had outgrown several large apartments and overflowed into the homes of his friends and family, but he carried on to the last as one of the most intrepid of the younger collectors of today.

George himself began painting in 1929 and after some encouragement and assistance on my part revealed a profound and genuine talent. As his painting progressed, he displayed how the specific moods of his musical compositions had given a vital form and emotional strength to his paintings. The intense, dynamic impulses of his music became the dominating force in his painting. He was a good student and as his talent began to assert itself he spent more and more time in the art galleries and museums. He permitted himself to become soaked in the culture of painting and made many visits to the various galleries and the studios of painters so that he could acquaint himself more fully with the different principles and techniques. The work of Rouault was especially close to him and he was constantly enthralled by the life and spirit that animated his work. He wanted his own pictures and music to possess the same breathtaking power and depth. He strove constantly to master the same bold combination of accessories that he possessed as a composer. In his various paintings and especially his portraits he tried for the precise contour that defined the form and constantly concerned himself with composition and color.

His paintings called for no special aesthetic theories or psychology. In his many drawings of various degrees of completion – and there are over a hundred – he demonstrated an amazing skill as a draughtsman. His constant application and the quantity of the works left behind him are a sufficient indication of his love and desire to contribute something truly important. As I observed his progress, I noticed especially how he tried to supply to his painting the same warmth, enthusiasm and power that characterized his music.

He was especially interested in people and portraiture and he had a decided talent for presenting a whole personality in a small sketch. This is shown in the studies of Adolph Lewisohn, Maurice Sterne and others. These studies, which were achieved in a few minutes, were later used as material for his painting in oil. In his self-portrait, 'Checked Sweater', he built up his forms with layer upon layer of pigment and the result is a highly dramatic painting of emotional effectiveness, rich and alive. In the portrait of 'Schoenberg' he has solved an extremely interesting plastic problem and achieved a dynamic, expressive painting. This canvas is not only intense and vivid but shows a distinct admiration and respect for his sitter. As a man richly gifted in both head and heart, he constantly tried to endow his models with a most sensitive rendering of their individual character.

Besides being an able draughtsman, he possessed a compelling and powerful line and was able to achieve results with the most economical of means. One has only to observe the exquisite drawings of 'Girl Reading', his brother 'Ira' and 'Henry Botkin', which could have been the work of Picasso or Dufy.

He always made me believe that painting was a little in advance of music in expressing ideas and moods. If he was interested in the modern trends in art it was because they had the same qualities as the music with which he was concerned. He once told me when we were discussing the French painter Rouault, 'I am keen for dissonance; the obvious bores me. The new music and the new art are similar in rhythm, they share a somber power and fine sentiment.'

George had an instinctive sense of art's creative process and was especially sensitive to rhythm. In quiet and reticent tones he has painted some still lifes and landscapes and though they did not come as easily as the portraits, they show a richness and solidity, together with a considerable amount of assurance. He worked in watercolor and in the study of 'My Studio – Folly Beach', I am struck by the extraordinary feeling of graphic and pictorial beauty. It seems to have been rendered with a childish, primitive violence and yet possesses an opulence of beauty.

In the painting of 'My Grandfather', his style was somewhat like folk art. Some of his paintings possess deep, sonorous tones, as the picture of 'Jerome Kern', which represents one of the highest summits of his achievements. The head seems to emerge from a cavern of shadows, each tone resounds like a note of music. Rhythm by Gershwin in music would have a definite place in his painting. He was trying to achieve a kind of 'melodic' painting, the sort which creates a harmonious relation between man and the world around him.

His work was never self-consciously modern and he always avoided distracting mannerisms and surface cleverness. In all his later work he had developed a mastery of his craft and even though he found time to create only small studies, they were never mere exercises but self-contained examples of art.

His brother Ira became enthusiastic about paintng at the same time and joined him in the new pursuit. It was common for friends to drop around to their penthouse and find each at his easel busily laying on color when they should have been completing a new score. George was so encouraged by the praise of many eminent artists that there were periods when his paints and brushes almost weaned him away from his music. When we lived on Folly Island near Charleston and George was busily engaged in writing *Porgy and Bess*, he would abandon his piano often to rush out and join me in painting the picturesque Negro shacks. He painted and made sketches during his travels and his sketch book and easel were always part of his baggage.

Any judgment on the art of George Gershwin at this time can represent little more than a personal opinion. There is no doubt that he would have won increasing recognition had he lived, and if he was not famous as a painter it was merely because his activities as a composer had not given him sufficient opportunity to paint. His work was at all times serious and not a composer's pastime and every effort showed an earnestness and sincere love. I am confident with time his talent might have flowered into something comparable to his genius as a composer. As Mr Frank Crowninshield says in his introduction to the catalogue of the Gershwin Exhibition, 'George had a way of regarding his painting and his music as almost interchangeable phenomena. They sprang, he felt, from the same Freudian elements in him, one emerging as sight, the other as sound. The first he shaped with a brush, the second with a goose-quill.'

To the world at large George Gershwin will always be known as one of the foremost exponents of modern American music. He also will be remembered as a man who possessed an almost feverish and unquenchable enthusiasm for the fine arts. It was evident on observing his posthumous one-man show which was held at the Marie Harriman Gallery in New York City, in December, 1937, that he aspired to equal his achievements as a composer. He was on his way to that goal and from tactile apperception he was able to move steadily toward a truly optical vision that would have enabled him to create a personal style in keeping with his temperament. The task that he was unable to bring to fruition bears the indelible imprint of his genius and personality. In the words of Henry McBride, the noted art critic, 'if the soul be great, all expressions emanating from that soul must be great'.

Henry Botkin, 'Painter and Collector', *George Gershwin*, Merle Armitage, ed. (New York, 1938), pp. 137–43

FRANK CROWNINSHIELD
(1872–1947)

The celebrated editor of the fashionable monthly, *Vanity Fair* for twenty-two years, Frank Crowninshield was among the first to publish the writings of Gertrude Stein (in 1917), and an early piece by an unknown actor-playwright named Noël Coward (1921). Also interested in what was then called 'modern art', Crowninshield was one of the founders of New York's Museum of Modern Art in 1929. He and Gershwin met frequently at parties in the latter twenties.

Among the modern painters whose works George Gershwin collected so prodigally and knowingly, he found his spirit in the most exact accord with that of Georges Rouault. He responded particularly to the Frenchman's breathtaking power; the almost barbaric cadences that infused his canvases. 'Oh,' he used to exclaim, 'if only I could put Rouault into music!'

As Rouault, more than any recorded painter, employed blue – a strong, almost acid blue – as an essential base for his pictures, the association, however remote, comes instantly to mind that the men were alike in their ability to impart beauty and organized rhythm to their respective rhapsodies in blue.

George had a way of regarding his painting and his music as almost interchangeable phenomena. They sprang he felt, from the same Freudian elements in him – one emerging as sight, the other as sound; the first to be shaped with a brush, the second with a goose-quill. There were, indeed, periods when the palette almost weaned him from the piano; when he willingly stopped composing to paint and only grudgingly stopped painting to compose.

He painted when and where he could; sporadically, sometimes

hastily, witness the well-conceived watercolor of his bedroom at Folly Island near Charleston – an interior hurriedly washed down in the throes of composing *Porgy and Bess*. His drawings, too, were avowedly impromptu in nature. The excellent little sketch of Maurice Sterne, for example, was the work of ten minutes time, as was also the impression of his brother, Ira – a drawing so sensitive that it might well have been the work of Jean Cocteau or Raoul Dufy. Furthermore, such portraits were drawn directly in pen and ink, without benefit of pencil. Painting with him was an *affaire de coeur*, never an *affaire de ménage*. If, in composing his music, the temptation – the necessity, even – of marrying Broadway to Carnegie Hall was often implicit in his task, no such compulsion ever impelled him at his easel.

He was thirty-one when he first knew the feel of a brush in his hand, and thirty-eight when he died. In all his days he received no instruction in art, save from his friend and cousin, Henry Botkin, the painter. Toward the end of his life he improved rapidly and consistently, both as draftsman and painter, so rapidly indeed that he had looked forward to 1938 as a period in which he would set aside music for painting.

What, indubitably, remains his best work was achieved in the last three years of his life. We have only to study the sound and convincing portrait of Arnold Schoenberg, the animated head of Jerome Kern, and the two self-portraits (the standing figure, in opera-hat – a successful solution of a difficult structural problem – or the head-and-shoulder likeness, in a checked sweater); and then compare them with his first portraits, in order to realize how signal his advancement had been, not only in knowledge but sensibility.

It is a matter for melancholy that his happy Odyssey as an artist was destined, in mid-channel, to find so sudden an end. But it is pleasant to remember that the nearer he sailed to the rim of the Shadow, the clearer became his vision, the deeper the waters of his spirit.

Frank Crowninshield, essay for posthumous exhibition of Gershwin's paintings and drawings at the Marie Harriman Gallery, 18 December 1937 to 4 January 1938

IX
Hollywood: The End

A financial failure, *Porgy and Bess* closed abruptly in Washington, DC on 21 March 1936 following a brief tour. While Gershwin had been working on his opera the musical centre of gravity shifted from Broadway to Hollywood, where the sophisticated film fluffs of Fred Astaire and Ginger Rogers gave a smart, new meaning to the concept of the film musical. During this unequalled renaissance the leading New York composers – Jerome Kern, Irving Berlin, Cole Porter, Richard Rodgers, Harold Arlen – left the Depression-racked musical theatre for films. After the fiascos of *Pardon My English* and *Let 'em Eat Cake* and *Porgy*'s quick close, the Gershwins decided in the spring of 1936 to join their friends in California.

It was not easy. Negotiations began in mid-February of 1936 and were finally resolved at the end of June, when the Gershwins signed a contract with RKO to write a score for Astaire and Rogers, with an option for another, if all went well.

It did not. The Hollywood consensus was hardly encouraging and Gershwin was compelled to reassure the studio by telegram, just before he and Ira Gershwin left for California on 10 August 1936: INCIDENTALLY RUMORS ABOUT HIGHBROW MUSIC RIDICULOUS STOP AM OUT TO WRITE HITS.

And he did.

GEORGE GERSHWIN

Hollywood has taken on quite a new color since our last visit six years ago. There are many people in the business who talk the language of smart show people . . . All the writingmen and tunesmiths get together in a way that is practically impossible in the East . . . We have many

friends here . . . so the social life has also improved lately . . . I've
seen a great deal of Irving Berlin and Jerome Kern at poker parties
and the feeling around is very *gemütlich*.

Letter to Max Dreyfus (his publisher), 3 December 1936

HENRY BOTKIN

George started out by liking Hollywood because of the novelty of the
place, but in the end he became cynical and George wasn't a cynical
person. He would say, 'Harry, look at this place – desert. Here they
drill a bigger hole and install a swimming pool. Finally, they build
a still larger, deeper hole and put up a house. It's unbelievable.'

Robert Kimball and Alfred Simon, *The Gershwins* (New York, 1973), p.
226

HAROLD ARLEN

He would drop by, ring the bell and dash for the piano, play. *Then*
he'd say hello. [The song was the just completed 'They Can't Take
That away from Me' for *Shall We Dance*. Arlen's wife improvised an
eight-bar counterpoint as he played it a second time.] He loved it and
every time he played it he asked Annie – in her little voice – to sing.

Edward Jablonski and Lawrence Stewart, *The Gershwin Years* (New York,
1958), p. 266

MERLE ARMITAGE

The richness of the Gershwin environment was remarkable. His home
was always full of friends . . . Harold Arlen, Yip Harburg, Moss
Hart, George Pallay, Lillian Hellman, Arthur Kober, Edward G.
Robinson were a few of the many . . . Arnold Schoenberg, that musical giant, came often for tennis . . . Paulette Goddard and George
seemed to be very attracted to each other. Paulette would emerge from
her cabana in the scantiest of bathing suits and lie à la Cleopatra along
the side of the pool. As she stretched out a languid hand to ruffle the

hair of the swimming George, the anatomical display was superb . . . Somewhere in this merry-go-round the young French actress Simone Simon played a part. Her specialty seemed to be the telephone. I have waited interminably for George to come from the phone, only to be told by him, 'I was just talking to Simone.'

Merle Armitage, *George Gershwin – Man and Legend* (New York, 1958), pp. 60–62

HAROLD ARLEN

. . . he wanted to marry Paulette Goddard.* We sat by his pool talking about it. She was a great girl, but George's life style was very free-wheeling. I knew that marriage would tie him down, so I told him that he would have to give up some of the freedom he had. He didn't say anything, because I knew – all of us knew – that he wanted to get married. But George was the kind of guy who would go first to one house and play a few songs, then go on to another and play some more, then to another and so on. He knew he couldn't do that if he were married. Yet there was that warmth and wistfulness in him too, and it all made for great internal conflicts. So it would have been very hard for George to change his life style from work, party-going, tennis, golf, long fast walks in the mountains.

Robert Kimball and Alfred Simon, *The Gershwins* (New York, 1973), p. 204

OSCAR LEVANT

Tennis was second in his interest only to the piano. His pursuit of this sport permitted a transferral of the desk motive† to the outdoors, represented by a dazzling array of shirts, shorts, slacks, shoes and a repertory of tropical beach robes of almost Oriental splendor . . . His absorption in tennis was so complete that part of his man Paul's‡ manifold duties was to volley with him in pre-game warm-ups.

Even exceeding George's passion for tennis was that of [Arnold] Schoenberg, who played with the scientific absorption of a man who

---

*At the time she was married to Chaplin, though few in Hollywood were aware of it.
†The reference is to a special work desk designed by Gershwin.
‡Paul Mueller, who worked for Gershwin from the mid-thirties until Gershwin's death.

wants to know what makes the ball tick (but not hit). The meeting of Schoenberg and Gershwin was an affectionate one and resulted, among other things, in a standing invitation for the older man to use the Gershwin court on a regular day each week . . .

On one occasion, after playing two vigorous sets, Schoenberg and his opponents were driven from the court by a sudden shower, taking refuge in a shelter where George and I joined them. The sixty-odd-year-old Schoenberg wiped his brow and said, half to himself, 'Somehow I feel tired. I can't understand it.' Then added suddenly, 'That's right. I was up at five this morning. My wife gave birth to a boy.'

'Why didn't you tell us before?' said George. 'Come inside, we'll drink a toast.'

We adjourned to the house, the glasses were filled, and George spoke touchingly of the event. As he was about to drink, George raised his glass and paused. 'Why don't you call him George? It's a lucky name.'

Schoenberg shook his head wearily. 'You're too late. I already have a son named George.'

Oscar Levant, *A Smattering of Ignorance* (New York, 1941), pp. 186–7

George was greatly intrigued and faintly annoyed by the abstruseness of the music I was writing,* so sharply different from his own. With a certain pride and even more aggression I displayed a completed piece one day, to which he responded after an examination, 'It looks so confused.'

'Didn't you know?' I retorted. 'I've just been offered the chair of confusion at U.C.L.A.'

Oscar Levant, *A Smattering of Ignorance* (New York, 1941), p. 185

One of the most memorable experiences I have ever had in music occurred during that California visit, when Mrs Elizabeth Sprague Coolidge sponsored the performance of the four Schoenberg quartets and the last group of Beethoven, played by the Kolisch ensemble. George, Ira and I were overjoyed by this opportunity, and all the music impressed us deeply.

We were all together on the tennis court one morning when the talk turned to the concert of the previous day.

---

*Levant was then studying composition with Schoenberg.

'I'd like to write a quartet some day' said George. 'But it will be something simple, like Mozart.' Schoenberg mistakenly interpreted Gershwin's typically irrelevant reflection as a comment on his work and answered, somewhat nettled, 'I'm not a simple man – and, anyway, Mozart was considered far from simple in his day.'

Oscar Levant, *A Smattering of Ignorance* (New York, 1941), p. 188

ARNOLD SCHOENBERG
(1874–1951)

Composer, theorist, teacher and painter, Arnold Schoen-berg was the founder of the 'Second Viennese School' (which included his prize pupils, Alban Berg and Anton Webern), conceiving what he called a 'method of compos-ing with twelve tones' (others call it 'atonal music'). The advent of the Nazis caused Schoenberg to leave Germany for the US, where he taught at the University of Califor-nia, in Los Angeles, and was a major influence on several young American composers. Gershwin admired his work but was not one of his followers.

Many musicians do not consider George Gershwin a serious composer. But they should understand, serious or not, he is a composer – that is, a man who lives in music and expresses everything, serious or not, because it is his native language. There are a number of composers, serious (as they believe) or not (as I know), who learned to add notes together. But they are serious on account of a perfect lack of humor and soul. It seems to me beyond doubt that Gershwin was an innovator. What he has done with rhythm, harmony and melody is not merely style. It is fundamentally different from the mannerism of many a serious composer. Such mannerism is based on artificial presumptions, which are gained by speculation and conclusions drawn from the fashions and aims current among contemporary composers at certain times. Such a style is a superficial union of devices applied to a minimum of idea . . . Such music could be taken to pieces and put together in a different way, and the result would be the same nothing-ness expressed by another mannerism. One could not do this with Gershwin's music. His melodies are not products of a combination, nor of a mechanical union, but they are units and could not therefore be taken to pieces. Melody, harmony and rhythm are not welded together, but cast . . . I know he is an artist and a composer; he expressed musical ideas; and they were new – as is the way in which he expressed them.

Arnold Schoenberg, 'George Gershwin', *George Gershwin*, Merle Armitage, ed. (New York, 1938), pp. 97–8

FRANCES GERSHWIN GODOWSKY

When we visited George in 1937 a few months before he was sick, he seemed in wonderful shape. We both* were so impressed. He had such vitality and he was taking brisk walks every day. George had always been so absorbed in his work, but he had had some analysis with Dr [Gregory] Zilboorg, and I felt when I saw him that he was coming into his own as a rounded person. Several times he said to us, 'I don't feel I've scratched the surface. I'm out here to make enough money with movies so I don't have to think of money any more. Because I just want to work on American music: symphonies, chamber music, opera. This is what I really want to do. I don't feel I've even scratched the surface.' He told Leo he wanted to start on a string quartet.

Robert Kimball and Alfred Simon, *The Gershwins* (New York, 1973), p. 214

MERLE ARMITAGE

George and I talked art. Or we talked music. One of the things we discussed was the string quartet on which he was working at the time . . . He talked of the form his quartet would take, a fast opening movement, followed by a very slow second movement, based on themes he had heard when visiting Folly Island off Carolina coast with DuBose Heyward. The sounds of the dominant themes were so insistent that

*She and her husband, Leopold Godowsky, Jun. (son of the pianist), visited Gershwin during the Christmas–New Year holidays, 1936–7

he had not bothered to write them down. 'It's going through my head all the time', George said, 'and as soon as I have finished scoring the next picture, I'm going to rent me a little cabin up in Coldwater Canyon, away from Hollywood, and get the damn thing on paper. It's about to drive me crazy, it's so damned full of ideas!'

Merle Armitage, *George Gershwin – Man and Legend* (New York, 1958), p. 77

ROUBEN MAMOULIAN

George was like a child. He had a child's innocence and imagination. He could look at the same thing ever so many times and yet see it anew every time he looked at it and enjoy it. I remember once we were playing tennis at his home in Beverly Hills. This was after George and Ira had written the score for an Astaire–Rogers picture which had in it the wistful song, 'No, no, you can't take that away from me' [sic]. Now, George took his tennis, as most things he did, close to heart. He was not a very good player – I was even worse. Still, whenever he missed the ball he was heartbroken – he would clutch the racket to his chest and moan, 'No-o, no-o!' Once, when he missed the ball and moaned 'No-o, no-o,' I sang out, 'You can't take that away from me!' George laughed with delight. So after that every time George missed and moaned 'No-o, no-o,' I came forth with a lusty 'You can't take that away from me!' We did it time and again – and every time George would burst into laughter as if it had never happened before.

Rouben Mamoulian, 'I Remember', *George Gershwin*, Merle Armitage, ed. (New York, 1938), p. 55

MILTON A. CAINE

(b. 1922)

The writer, journalist and critic, Caine interviewed Nathaniel Shilkret in 1951 for a book he was working on. Shilkret was an old friend of Gershwin – and an executive at RCA Victor Recordings he made the first recording of *An American in Paris* soon after its première. In 1935 he went to Hollywood; when the Gershwins arrived he was musical director at RKO and worked closely with Gershwin on *Shall We Dance* and *A Damsel in Distress*.

Shilkret, as conductor of the studio orchestra for RKO, saw Gershwin continually during the last three months of his life. They worked together on this picture which was 'a horrible mixup for George'. The story was vague. Mark Sandrich, the director, wanted another *American* for a ballet finale. George came in with something in Latin–American tempo, which no one cared for. Astaire and Sandrich ganged up on Gershwin for a better ballet; gave him a hard time. Shilkret often wondered why Gershwin didn't walk out on them but Gershwin was always 'very sweet'.

A new idea for the ballet was to use Tommy Dorsey's orchestra which was being used to augment the studio orchestra as part of the finale. *Shall We Dance?* was suggested as a title for the picture, and Gershwin wrote the song. He also wrote one called 'Wake up, brothers'* to be part of the ballet; it was never used. By this time he didn't know what they wanted – neither did anyone else. He said he'd write anything they wanted. ('Wake up, brothers' had been thrown out). George and Ira used to work till 2 a.m. trying to fashion something for them. George often complained about not feeling well.

Milton A. Caine, interview with Nathaniel Shilkret, 1 May 1951

*'Wake up, brother and dance'

HENRY BOTKIN

The last year of his life was an awful year. Did you know about the awful loneliness he had? I remember once he came right out with it and said, 'Harry, this year I've GOT to get married.' Just like that. Like saying he had to write a new opera or something. The truth is George wanted the most beautiful gal, the most marvelous hostess, someone interested in music. What he wanted and demanded just didn't exist.

Robert Kimball and Alfred Simon, *The Gershwins* (New York, 1973), p. 216

DAVID EWEN
(1907–85)

Author, editor and teacher, David Ewen was a prolific writer. He produced dozens of volumes, especially about American popular song and songwriters. He compiled various encyclopaedias on different aspects of music, including the *Complete Book of the American Musical Theater* (1958) and *Encyclopedia of Concert Music* (1959); among his biographies are studies of Irving Berlin, Toscanini, Jerome Kern and Leonard Bernstein, with no less than three on Gershwin.

Then he fell in love – or thought he did. At a . . . Hollywood party he met Paulette Goddard, then married to Charlie Chaplin . . . He was deaf to the advice of his closest friends who tried to convince him that such a marriage would not work out for him. A turbulent love affair during the next few weeks absorbed him completely . . . her refusal to leave Chaplin was a blow that shook him to his very roots . . . One day he asked Alexander Steinert,* 'I am thirty-eight, famous, and rich, but profoundly unhappy. Why?'

David Ewen, *George Gershwin – His Journey to Greatness* (Englewood Cliffs, NJ), pp. 276–7

*Composer, conductor and arranger, he studied with Charles Martin Loeffler in Boston and Vincent d'Indy in Paris. He served as vocal coach for the original production of *Porgy and Bess* and conducted several performances during the opera's tour.

Although family and friends attributed Gershwin's uncharacteristic behavior to his reaction to Hollywood, he was in fact seriously ill. This first surfaced in February 1937 during a rehearsal with the Los Angeles Philharmonic. While conducting selections from *Porgy and Bess* he suddenly tottered. Paul Mueller, his associate-assistant, feared he was about to fall and rushed to the podium. But, recovered, Gershwin assured him that all was well and that for a moment he had lost his balance. The rehearsal continued without further incident and the near-fainting spell was forgotten. But that evening, during a performance of the Concerto in F, he suffered a blackout briefly, during which he fumbled one passage and later mentioned that he thought he had smelled burning rubber. Concerned, he decided to see a physician, who found nothing, and Gershwin chose to ignore the incidents. A couple of months later he experienced another moment of dizziness and the strange, unpleasant, odor; it was so fleeting that Gershwin, in the light of his February physical examination, dismissed it. By June, however, he began to complain of blinding headaches, was snappishly fretful and uncharacteristically enervated. Gershwin, it was evident, was suffering from more than a neurotic response to Hollywood.

OSCAR LEVANT

Though he had played the Concerto dozens of times in public with great fluency I noticed that he stumbled on a very easy passage in the first movement. Then, in the andante, in playing the four simple octaves that conclude the movement above sustained orchestral chords, he blundered again. When I went backstage, he greeted me with the curious remark, 'When I made those mistakes I was thinking of you, you . . .', concluding with some gruffly uncomplimentary characterization.

Oscar Levant, *A Smattering of Ignorance* (New York, 1941), p. 198

S. N. BEHRMAN

We* went over to the Gershwin's. Lee† and Ira greeted us . . .
George came downstairs accompanied by a male nurse. I stared at
him. It was not the George we all knew. He was very pale. The light
had gone from his eyes. He seemed old. He greeted me mirthlessly.
His handshake was limp, the spring had gone out of his walk. He
came to the sofa near where I was sitting and lay down on it. He tried
to adjust his head against the pillow. The nurse hovered over him.

I asked him if he felt pain.

'Behind my eyes,' he said, and repeated it: 'behind my eyes.' I knelt
beside him on the sofa and put my hand under his head. I asked if
he felt like playing the piano. He shook his head. It was the first
refusal I'd ever heard from him.

'I had to live for this,' he said, 'that Sam Goldwyn should say to
me: "Why don't you write hits like Irving Berlin?" '

S. N. Behrman, *People in a Diary* (Boston, 1972), p. 253

OSCAR LEVANT

For one of the few occasions in my experience, George was genuinely
offended when the composition of the score for the *Goldwyn Follies*
had progressed almost to the point of completion. The producer sum-
moned him to a conference one afternoon and insisted that the performance of the music be given in the presence of his full staff of loyal
well-paid amanuenses (stooges) . . . The experience of thus submitting
his work for the approbation of a dummy panel, whose opinion was
as predictable as the result of a Jersey City election, humiliated George
– who felt that this stage of his career had long since passed.

Oscar Levant, *A Smattering of Ignorance* (New York, 1941) pp. 196–7

---

*With him were Oscar Levant and Sonya Levien, the screen writer, who collaborated with
Gut Bolton on the Gershwin's *Delicious* and wrote the screenplay for *Rhapsody in Blue*
(1945).
†Leonore Strunsky Gershwin, Ira Gershwin's wife.

S. N. BEHRMAN

The next afternoon I went to the Gershwins'. I saw Paul [Mueller] George's . . . butler, whom I had known in New York. He had driven George to his new domain.* I asked him how George had behaved.

'He was all right,' said Paul, 'till we got to the house.'

'What happened then?'

'He asked for a dark room. I darkened the room for him – pulled all the shades down – made it quite dark. Then he asked for a towel to put over his eyes.'

S. N. Behrman, *People in a Diary* (Boston, 1972), pp. 254–5

RICHARD RODGERS

(1902–79)

> A composer and lyricist, Richard Rodgers studied at the Institute of Musical Art (now the Juilliard School of Music). From 1920 until 1942 he collaborated in song-writing with Lorenz Hart, and they produced musicals such as *On Your Toes*, *Babes in Arms* and *Pal Joey*. Following Hart's death, Rodgers teamed up with Oscar Hammerstein, beginning with the historic *Oklahoma!* in 1943, and ending with *The Sound of Music* in 1959. Following Hammerstein's death, Rodgers continued in two unsuccessful collaborations with lyricists Martin Charnin and Stephen Sondheim.

I don't like what I hear about George. He's had a complete mental collapse and they don't know what to do with him. They'd like to send him East to a sanitarium as they don't trust the ones out here, but he's too ill to be moved. Moss [Hart] tells me he can't eat or even talk and is in a house which they've taken for him and turned into a hospital.

Richard Rodgers, *Musical Stages* (New York, 1975), p. 182: Letter to Dorothy Rodgers

*Gershwin was moved from his home on Roxbury Drive to the nearby home of lyricist E. Y. Harburg, who was leaving for New York.

GEORGE A. PALLAY

(1900–1979)

One of the more elusive members of the Gershwin circle, even regarding his name. He is identified as having a brother named Max Abrahamson and was a cousin of Lou Paley, who undoubtedly introduced him to Gershwin. An entrepreneur, Pallay was a stockbroker; in the late 1930s he had a construction business and was active in the renovation of the grand houses in Beverly Hills. No musician, he shared Gershwin's interest in women. He was not popular with the Gershwin family.

Four weeks ago [c. early June] he seemed unhappy and a bit moody. He was critical of things, people, events. I was around with him constantly and he always spoke his heart out to me. Then he complained of headaches and fatigue. Immediately doctors examined him at home very thoroughly, as thorough as a home examination can be. Every part of him was checked and found OK.

George A. Pallay, letter, after 11 July 1937, to Irene Gallagher, secretary to Gershwin's publisher, Max Dreyfus

MORTON L. KASDAN, MD

(b. 1936)

A physician and surgeon, practising medicine in Louisville, Kentucky, he specializes in hand surgery. He is associated with the Humana Hospital Suburban.

Headaches, which were initially dismissed as psychosomatic, began in June. Gershwin felt they were a result of exhaustion and overwork. Dr Ernst Simmel, a psychoanalyst in Los Angeles, was consulted. He felt that Gershwin's illness was organic in nature and referred him to Dr Gabriell Segall, an internist. The first consultation with Dr Segall took place June 9, 1937. Gershwin's presenting complaints were headaches and dizzy spells. The episodes of headaches were usually in the early morning hours. The dizzy spells were about 30 seconds in duration and associated with olfactory hallucinations. These symptoms developed at least once daily, often in situations involving stress. No abnormalities were found on physical examination.

Morton L. Kasdan, MD, *Journal of the Kentucky Medical Association*, November 1987, p. 650

LOUIS CARP, MD
(1893–1979)

A graduate of the Columbia University College of Physicians and Surgeons (1915), Louis Carp taught surgery at Columbia, with a special interest in geriatric surgery, about which he wrote a great deal. He was also interested in the arts and music, and after his retirement he began writing a book about famous composers who died before the age of forty. These included Gershwin, Bellini and Mozart.

At 2:45 in the afternoon of June 23, 1937, internist Dr Gabriell Segall, admitted him to Cedars of Lebanon Hospital in Los Angeles with a history of severe, pounding headaches of two weeks' duration. The headaches were localized in the frontal and temporal regions, worse in the morning, occasionally associated with dizziness and nausea; he also had a recurrence of the olfactory hallucinations of a very foul odor.

He was listless and had impaired coordination. A fork would involuntarily drop from his hand when it was erratically directed toward his mouth; water spilled from a glass which shook in his unsteady hands; his car threaded in and out of traffic when he was at the wheel; he also exhibited eccentric fingering at the piano keyboard. He swayed, he stumbled on stairs and lacked his usual physical stamina.

There were two abrupt and illogical episodes that were startling. Riding in his car driven by Paul Mueller, his majordomo, George suddenly opened the door and tried to push Mueller out.

'What are you trying to do, kill us?' demanded the shaken Mueller. The answer was, 'I don't know.'

Another time, his fingers crushed chocolates that had been sent him and then he used the mess as a body ointment.* On examination by

*A gift from his sister-in-law, Leonore, Mrs Ira Gershwin.

neurologist, Dr Eugene Ziskind, he was found to have photophobia, a blood pressure of 100/70, normal reflexes and ocular findings, and no tangible evidence of organic lesions. . . . Gershwin was discharged on June 26 with a final note on the record 'most likely hysteria'.

Louis Carp, MD, *The American Journal of Surgical Pathology*, October 1979, pp. 474–5

GEORGE A. PALLAY

All during this period there were days when he indicated [he was] on the way to recovery. This by fewer headaches; moments of cheerfulness, clear thinking, planning for his comfort and work. Always most optimistic of not only his recovery but the fact that nothing physical was the matter . . .

Then came Friday 9 July . . . Ira and I found George asleep . . . the first one without pillows to relieve headaches . . . At seven p.m., when he was escorted to the bath-room, he suddenly shook and trembled all over. He was bedded immediately and his eyes seemed to swell. Doctors, brain and otherwise rushed to the house, removed him after examination to the hospital at midnight.*

George A. Pallay, letter to Irene Gallagher

LOUIS CARP

Neurosurgeon Dr [Carl W.] Rand, suggested an additional consultation. Emil Mosbacher, a New York stockbroker . . . was a close friend of George. Leonore Gershwin . . . telephoned Mosbacher from Beverly Hills to contact an outstanding neurosurgeon to fly to the hospital for urgent consultation. Mosbacher telephoned the famous Boston neurosurgeon, Dr Harvey Cushing. Cushing stated that he had retired from operative surgery and recommended Dr Walter E. Dandy, Professor of Neurosurgery at Johns Hopkins Medical School in Baltimore. Mosbacher found that Dr Dandy was 'at sea', but through a radio broadcast located him on a yacht in Chesapeake Bay, a guest of Governor Harry W. Nice of Maryland. Mosbacher was

*In a coma, Gershwin was admitted to the Cedars of Lebanon Hospital, Los Angeles.

constantly on the telephone in his home in White Plains, coordinating available information. The Coast Guard brought Dr Dandy to shore where a police escort preceded him [to the nearest airport]. Here Mosbacher arranged for a private American Airlines plane to fly Dr Dandy to Newark Airport in order to emplane for Los Angeles. In a three-way conversation with the doctors at Cedars of Lebanon Hospital and Mosbacher, Dr Dandy was told that immediate surgery was mandatory. His trip was called off.

Louis Carp, MD, *The American Journal of Surgical Pathology*, October 1979, p. 475

GEORGE A. PALLAY

George was taken to the operating room at twelve-thirty Saturday night our time. I was installed at a desk ten feet away from the room. The family were forced to wait on the fourth floor and their only contact were their phone talks to me. Of the twenty or twenty-five people cooperating in the work, I was able to talk constantly with the nurses, internees, doctors, etc. Of course I asked thousands of questions.

George A. Pallay, letter to Irene Gallagher

LOUIS CARP

Meantime, Dr Howard C. Nafziger, Professor of Neurosurgery, University of California Medical School, had been located on vacation in Lake Tahoe in Nevada.

Louis Carp, MD, *The American Journal of Surgical Pathology*, October 1979, p. 475

MORTON L. KASDAN

Dr Rand, with Drs Nafziger, Segall and Ziskind attending, performed the surgery . . . The operation lasted approximately four hours. Gershwin never regained consciousness, and died several hours later, on July 11, 1937, at 10.35 a.m.

Morton L. Kasdan, MD, *Journal of the Kentucky Medical Association*, November 1987, p. 651

GEORGE A. PALLAY

I could not get myself to tell them that it was all hopeless. I did tell Lee Gershwin that even if he lived he could expect at its best that George's left side of face and arm, side and leg would be forever paralyzed, that he'd never be able to play again.

George A. Pallay, letter to Irene Gallagher

WALTER E. DANDY
(1886–1946)

A neurosurgeon, Walter Dandy was noted for the introduction of the techniques ventriculography and encephalography (which made possible the more accurate diagnosis and localization of brain tumours). He also developed new instruments for surgical procedures. In 1937 he was Professor of Neurosurgery at the Johns Hopkins Medical School, Baltimore, Maryland.

I do not see what more could have been done for Mr Gershwin. It was just one of those fulminating tumors. There are not many tumors that have uncinate attacks that are removeable, and it would be my impression that although the tumor in large part might have been extirpated and he would have recovered for a little while, it would have recurred very quickly, since the whole thing fulminated so suddenly at the onset. I think the outcome is much the best for himself, for a man as brilliant as he with a recurring tumor would have been terrible; it would have been a slow death.

Dr Walter A. Dandy, extract, letter to Dr Gabriell Segall

OSCAR HAMMERSTEIN II

(1895–1960)

Our friend wrote music
And in that mould he created
Gaiety and sweetness and beauty
And twenty-four hours after he had gone
His music filled the air
And in triumphant accents
Proclaimed to this world of men
That gaiety and sweetness and beauty
Do not die . . .

Oscar Hammerstein II, 'To George Gershwin', George Gershwin Memorial Concert, Hollywood Bowl, 8 September 1937

Appendix: Gershwin on Music

Gershwin's success made him a popular subject for newspaper and periodical articles, interviews and, following
the stunning impact of the *Rhapsody in Blue*, he was asked
to write articles about his work and music in general. He
was most frequently questioned about 'jazz' (or rather what
at the time was considered jazz), its influence on American
music, popular song, and his own future plans.

On Music

[To Gershwin of the greatest importance in music were] ideas and
feeling. The various tonalities and sounds mean nothing unless they
grow out of ideas. Not many composers have ideas . . . Whoever has
inspired ideas will write the great music of our period . . . I don't
think there is any such thing as mechanized musical composition
without feeling, without emotions. Music is one of the arts which
appeals directly through the emotions . . . The composer has to do
every bit of his work himself. Hard work can never be replaced in
the composition of music. If music ever became machine-made in that
sense, it would cease to be an art.

George Gershwin, 'The Composer in the Machine Age', *Revolt in the Arts*,
Oliver Saylor, ed. (New York, 1930); reprinted in *George Gershwin*, Merle
Armitage, ed. (New York, 1938), pp. 225–230

Making music is actually little else than a matter of invention aided
and abetted by emotion. In composing we combine what we know of
music with what we feel. To my mind all artists are a combination of
two elements – the heart and the brain. Some composers overdo one
of the elements in their work. Tchaikovsky – although he was a good
technician – was apt to stress the heart too much; Berlioz was all mind.
Now Bach was that glorious example of the unity of the two . . .

To me feeling counts more than anything else, more than technique or knowledge. Of course, feeling by itself, without certain other attributes, is not enough, but it is the supreme essential.

Edward Jablonski, 'Gershwin on Music', *Musical America*, July 1962, p. 33

Unquestionably modern musical America has been influenced by modern musical Europe, but it seems to me that modern European composers, in turn, have very largely received their stimulus, their rhythms and impulses from Machine Age America. They have an older tradition of musical technique which has helped them put into musical terms a little more clearly the thoughts that originated here. They can express themselves more glibly.

George Gershwin, 'The Composer in the Machine Age'; reprinted in *George Gershwin*, Merle Armitage, ed. (New York, 1938), p. 225

Musical Semantics

Jazz is a word which has been used for at least five or six types of music. It is really a conglomeration of many things. It has a little bit of ragtime, the blues, classicism and spirituals. Basically, it is a matter of rhythm. After rhythm in importance come intervals . . . intervals which are peculiar to the rhythm. After all, there is nothing new in music.

George Gershwin, 'The Composer in the Machine Age', *George Gershwin*, Merle Armitage, ed. (New York, 1938), p. 227

The same word-trouble surrounds the colloquial use of the phrase 'classical music'. It means as many things as there are people to say it. A man writes a piece of music which he considers serious, but which is pretty awful; he labels his work 'classic' and an unsuspecting public accepts the label . . . From any sound critical standpoint, labels mean nothing at all. Good music is good music, even if you call it 'oysters'.

George Gershwin, 'Mr Gershwin Replies to Mr Kramer', *Singing*, October 1926, pp. 17–18

. . . if you were in Europe and heard the music of our supposedly native composers, you would be unable to say 'that work is American.' They no more voice the spirit of these United States than did Tchaikovsky represent Russia, or Puccini Italy, when they wrote in the styles of other lands. Do you know, I think Irving Berlin is more typically American than many of those whose works are heard in opera and concert halls.

George Gershwin, ' "Swanee" and Its Author', *Along Broadway – the Edison Musical Magazine*, October 1920, p. 9

Folk Music and Jazz

The great music of the past in other countries has always been built on folk-music. This is the strongest source of musical fecundity. America is no exception among the countries. It is not always recognized that America has folk-music; yet it really has not only one but many different folk-musics. It is a vast land and different sorts of folk-music have sprung up in different parts, all having validity, and all being a possible foundation for development into art-music. For this reason, I believe that it is possible for a number of distinctive styles to develop in America, all legitimately born of folk-song from different localities. Jazz, ragtime, Negro spirituals and blues, Southern mountain songs, country fiddling and cowboy songs can all be employed in the creation of American art music, and are actually used by many composers now. These composers are certain to produce something worthwhile if they have the innate feeling and talent to develop the rich material offered to them. There are also other composers who can be classed as legitimately American who do not make use of folk-music as a base, but who have personally, working in America, developed highly individualized styles and methods. Their newfound materials should be called American just as an invention is called American if it is made by an American!

George Gershwin, 'The Relation of Jazz to American Music', *American Composers on American Music*, Henry Cowell, ed. (Stanford, 1933), p. 186

Let jazz speak for itself. It is here, and all the tirades of our musical jeremiahs cannot take it from us or abate its profound influence on the music of the present and future. There has been too much argument about jazz – most of it from people who are not even clear in their terminology. To condemn jazz, for example, because there is much bad jazz in the world is as absurd as to condemn all music because much bad music exists. I hold no brief for those compositions of the Dada school, which employ the instrumentation of electric fans or couple fifty synchronized pianos in a riot of noisy cacophony. That is not jazz; it is merely delirium. But if you take the best of our modern serious jazz and study it, you can come to only one conclusion – that it is, in the words of Madame d'Alvarez: 'America's greatest contribution to the musical art.'

George Gershwin, 'Does Jazz Belong to Art?', *Singing*, July 1926, p. 13

Jazz I regard as an American folk-music; not the only one, but a very powerful one which is probably in the blood and feeling of the American people more than any other style of folk-music. I believe that it can be made the basis of serious symphonic works of lasting value, in the hands of a composer with talent for both jazz and symphonic music.

George Gershwin, 'The Relation of Jazz to American Music', *American Composers on American Music*, Henry Cowell, ed. (Stanford, 1933), p. 187

The late Amy Lowell, the great New England poet and seer, was one of those who loved jazz, although she could neither sing it nor play it nor dance it. 'I can only move my toe to it', she told me once, 'but if I couldn't do that, I think I should burst with the rapture of it.'

George Gershwin 'Does Jazz Belong to Art?', *Singing*, July 1926, p. 14

The only kinds of music which endure are those which possess form in the universal sense and folk music. All else dies. But unquestionably folk songs are being written and have been written which contain enduring elements of jazz. To be sure, that is only an element; it is not the whole. An entire composition written in jazz could not live.

George Gershwin, 'The Composer in the Machine Age', *George Gershwin*, Merle Armitage, ed. (New York, 1938), p. 277

American popular music, since its origin, has been steadily gaining in originality; today it may truly lay claim to being the most vital of contemporary popular music. Unfortunately however, most songs die at an early age and are soon completely forgotten by the self-same public that once sang them with gusto. The reason for this is that they are sung and played too much when they were alive, and cannot stand the strain of their very popularity.

George Gershwin, Introduction, *George Gershwin's Song-book* (New York, 1932), p. ix

Musical Techniques

Many of us have learned to write music by studying the most successful songs published. But imitation can go only so far. The young song writer may start by imitating a successful composer he admires, but he must break away as soon as he has learned the maestro's technique . . . the study of musical technique is indispensable. Many people say that too much study kills spontaneity in music, but although study may kill a small talent, it must develop a big one. In other words, if study kills a musical endowment, that endowment deserves to be killed.

George Gershwin, Introduction, *Tin Pan Alley*, Isaac Goldberg (New York, 1930), pp. ix-x

Bach's Passacaglia was a great piece of music before Stokowski orchestrated it. Rimsky-Korsakov reorchestrated in great measure Mussorgsky's Boris Godunov. Chopin, although one of the world's greatest musicians, was a notably poor orchestrator. The ability to orchestrate is a talent apart from the ability to create. The world is full of competent orchestrators who cannot for the life of them write four bars of original music.

George Gershwin, 'Mr Gershwin Replies to Mr Kramer', *Singing*, October 1926, pp. 17–18

I've never really studied musical form. That's nothing, of course, to be proud of. But regardless of the kind of music a composer is writing, it must have a definite line of progression. It must have a beginning and an end and a suitable section combining the two, just as the human body, to be complete, must have arms, legs, and a head. In this sense of trying to make my musical compositions each a complete work, I suppose there is a certain form to them.

Hyman Sandow, 'Gershwin to Write New Rhapsody', *Musical America*, 18 February 1928, p. 5

Composing at the piano is not a good practice. But I started that way and it has become a habit. However, it is possible to give the mind free rein and use the piano only to try what you can hear mentally. The best method is one which will not permit anything to hold you down in any way, for it is always easier to think in a straight line without the distraction of sounds. The mind should be allowed to run loose, unhampered by the piano, which may be used now and then to stimulate thought and set an idea aflame.

George Gershwin, Introduction, *Tin Pan Alley*, Isaac Goldberg (New York, 1930), pp. viii-ix

The Jazz Age

. . . American life is nervous, hurried, syncopated, ever accelerando, and slightly vulgar. I should use the word vulgar without intent of offense. There is a vulgarity that is newness. It is essential. The Charleston is vulgar, but it has a strength, an earthiness, that is an essential part of symphonic sound.

George Gershwin, 'Jazz is the Voice of the American Soul', *Theatre Magazine*, June 1926, p. 52B

Almost every great composer profoundly influences the age in which he lives. Bach, Beethoven, Wagner, Brahms, Debussy, Stravinsky. They have all recreated something of their time so that millions of people could feel it more forcefully and better understand their time . . . The composer who writes music for himself and doesn't want it to be heard is generally a bad composer.

George Gershwin, 'The Composer in the Machine Age', *George Gershwin*, Merle Armitage, ed. (New York, 1938), p. 229

An Ideal Concert

First the Bach Passacaglia, orchestrated by Stokowski. Then, a symphony by Mozart or Beethoven, preferably the latter's Fifth or Seventh. I'd want Stravinsky on the program too, represented by either his 'Petrouchka' or 'Le sacre du printemps'. And I'd wind up the concert with Richard Strauss' 'Till Eulenspiegel'. As alternate pieces

I'd like to hear Debussy's 'L'après-midi d'un faune' or one of Bach's Brandenberg Concertos.

Hyman Sandow, 'Gershwin to Write New Rhapsody', *Musical America*, 18 February 1928, p. 5

On His Own Compositions

Rhapsody in Blue (1924)

The *Rhapsody in Blue* represents what I have been striving for since my earliest composition. I wanted to show that jazz is an idiom not to be limited to a mere song and chorus that consumed three minutes in presentation . . . I succeeded in showing that jazz is not merely a dance, it comprises bigger themes and purposes.

George Gershwin, 'Jazz is the Voice of the American Soul', *Theatre Magazine*, June 1926, p. 52B

In the *Rhapsody* I tried to express our manner of living, the tempo of living, the tempo of our modern life with its speed and chaos and vitality . . . I consider the *Rhapsody* as embodying an assimilation of feeling rather than presenting specific scenes from American life in music.

Hyman Sandow, 'Gershwin to Write New Rhapsody', *Musical America*, 18 February 1928, p. 5

When I wrote the *Rhapsody in Blue* I took the 'blues' and put them in a larger and more serious form. That was twelve years ago and the *Rhapsody in Blue* is still very much alive, whereas if I had taken the same themes and put them in songs they would have been gone years ago.

George Gershwin, 'Rhapsody in Catfish Row', *New York Times*, 20 October 1935

Concerto in F (1925)

My greatest musical thrill? The time that I first heard my Concerto in F played by an orchestra. That was my first orchestration you know. Two weeks before the concerto was publicly presented . . . I hired an orchestra of fifty musicians with whom I played the piece in the Globe Theater. That was an experience I guess I'll never forget.

Hyman Sandow, 'Gershwin to Write New Rhapsody', *Musical America*, 18 February 1928, p. 5

Walter Damrosch asked me to write something for his New York Symphony Orchestra. This showed great confidence on his part, as I had never written a symphony before. I started to write the concerto in London, after buying four or five books on musical structure to find out what the concerto form actually was! And, believe me, I had to come through – because I had already signed a contract to play it seven times. It took me three months to compose this concerto, and one month to orchestrate it. Because it was my first symphonic work, I was so anxious to hear it that I engaged fifty-five musicians to read it for me . . . and you can imagine my delight when it sounded just as I had planned.

George Gershwin, *New York Tribune*, 29 November 1925

Mr Kramer does me an injustice in stating that my piano concerto was orchestrated by anyone but myself. The *Rhapsody in Blue* was orchestrated by Ferdie Grofé, but this was done because the Whiteman orchestra is such a unique combination. And yet Mr Grofé worked from a very complete piano and orchestral sketch, in which many of the orchestral colors were indicated . . . But the concerto was orchestrated entirely by myself.

George Gershwin, 'Mr Gershwin Answers Mr Kramer', *Singing*, October 1926, pp. 17–18

An American in Paris (1928)

This new piece, really a rhapsodic ballet, is written very freely and is the most modern music I've yet attempted. The opening part will be developed in typical French style, in the manner of Debussy and the Six, though the themes are all original. My purpose here is to portray the impression of an American visitor in Paris as he strolls about the city, listens to the various street noises, and absorbs the French atmosphere.

Hyman Sandow, 'Gershwin Presents a New Work', *Musical America*, 18 August 1928, p. 5

Second Rhapsody

. . . have finished fifty-five pages of the orchestration of my new Rhapsody and, in about another week, I expect to finish the entire thing. I have an idea it is going to sound very good as I have made quite a rich orchestration. I am going to call it *Second Rhapsody* instead of the title I had in California.* I think it is much simpler and more dignified.

George Gershwin, letter to George Pallay, 19 May 1931

Porgy and Bess

It was my idea that opera should be entertaining – that it should contain all the elements of entertainment. Therefore, when I chose *Porgy and Bess*, a tale of Charleston Negroes, for a subject, I made sure that it would enable me to write light as well as serious music and that it would enable me to include humor as well as tragedy – in fact, all of the elements of entertainment for the eye as well as the ear.

George Gershwin, 'Rhapsody in Catfish Row', *New York Times*, 20 October 1935

My work is done almost exclusively at night, and my best is achieved in the fall and winter months. A beautiful spring or summer day is least conducive to making music, for I prefer the outdoors to the work. I don't write at all in the morning, for the obvious reason that I am not awake at the time. The afternoon I devote to physical labor – orchestrations, piano copies, etc. At night, when other people are asleep or out for a good time, I can get absolute quiet for my composing. Not that perfect peace is always necessary; often I have written my tunes with people in the same room or playing cards in the next. If I find myself in the desired mood I can hold it until I finish the song.

George Gershwin, Introduction, *Tin Pan Alley*, Isaac Goldberg (New York, 1930), p. ix

Rhapsody in Rivets.

Index

Figures in *italics* refer to illustrations.